SMOKE & MIRRORS
Most of the Real Thing – 1066-1946

Kenneth Cartwright

Copyright © 2015 K.Cartwright
All rights reserved.

SMOKE & MIRRORS:
Most Of The Real Thing – 1066-1946

Section:	Page No
One: Observations In A Cynical World	6
Two: The Prime Phobia Of Establishments – Rebellion	8
Three: When Organised Tyranny Began In England	11
Four: Regency-Papacy Unions	13
Five: The 'Order Of The Garter' Prevails	21
Six: Pioneering Public Control Tactics In Britain	22
Seven: Keeping All Of The Minions In Ignorance	27
Eight: Malignant Catholicism – On The Back Of Empire Builders	32
Nine: Weapons And Palaces	34
Ten: Henry 8th In The Face Of The Founder Of Propaganda	38
Eleven: Papacy Struggles In The Lands Of Europe 'To-Be'	38
Twelve: Notorious Social Class and Gender Divisions	48
Thirteen: The First National Civil War In Europe	50

Section:	Page No
Fourteen: War Ethics And Legacies	54
Fifteen: Reformation Struggles	58
Sixteen: The First Nations Of Europe	64
Seventeen: The Birth Of Literary Grapevines	68
Eighteen: American Slaves And British Production	73
Nineteen: The British Empire – Some You Win, Some You Lose	77
Twenty: While The French Sorted Themselves Out	80
Twenty One: Britain: The Evil State	86
Twenty Two: Anything To Rid Europe Of Napoleon Bonaparte	90
Twenty Three: War Economics	96
Twenty Four: With Bonaparte Gone, The Revival Of Holiness	101
Twenty Five: Quell The Rebellion – Again	104
Twenty Six: A Remarkable Coup For The European Aristocracy	106
Twenty Seven The Control Of Foreign Minions	108
Twenty Eight: Insane Adventurism	115
Twenty Nine: British Industrial Hell	118

Section:	Page No
Thirty:	
The Crimean War	127
Thirty One:	
Evolving Protestants	133
Thirty Two:	
Opening The Vast Lands	137
Thirty Three:	
Minion Deceptions Abound	140
Thirty Four:	
Germany And Italy Evolve	143
Thirty Five:	
Africa Subdued	150
Thirty Six:	
Steel	156
Thirty Seven:	
British Philanthropy And Charity	159
Thirty Eight:	
Preludes Of The Great War	163
Thirty Nine:	
Dreadnaughts Mania	167
Forty:	
Hoodwinking Abound - The British Establishment Ignores Its Minions	171
Forty One:	
The Great War – Between Establishments, But Not Between Minions	174
Forty Two:	
British Women Acclaimed	179
Forty Three:	
The Eventual Demise Of The USA – European Destitution	182
Forty Four:	
Spain And Poland Compared	188
Forty Five:	
The Ominous Iron Curtain – Of Churchill's Making	194

SMOKE & MIRRORS is concluded within 'Volume Two', soon to be completed. In the meantime, I sincerely hope that the information included in this volume, grips you enough to spur you into volume two. I am determined not to disappoint. Truly, the 21st century is evolving dramatically and traumatically, to the extent maybe, where only those that venture 'out of the box' cope, within Europe and within the rest of the world, for that matter. Striving to keep you ahead. Have a good read.

Regards: Kenneth Cartwright

Section One:
Observations In A Cynical World

I was circumstantially politically radicalised as a boy, due to my father's manic approach to life. Then, inevitably influenced by him in the midst of his frequent rants, I was also influenced by international events because he always brought them to the forefront within our household. Most were profound, but more particularly they also often corroborated his contentions and they strengthened his 'communistic' inclinations. Russian Migs ruling the skies during the 1950s Korean war, the appearance of Sputnik and the most distinctive human icon of the early 1960s, Yuri Gagarin, the first man to orbit the earth in space. Then, I had no broad conceptions. All of the world to me – due to my father's perspective of life – was a 'political' maelstrom, continuously revitalised by the prominent personalities of the day. Then it was all about Nakita Kruschev thumping his fists at Dwight Eisenhower over the Gary Powers incident. Skulduggery and ferocity in the twilight of the new nuclear – Armageddon – age, in the wake of the Hiroshima and Nagasaki atrocities. In my home, the Americans were the true villains.

Now, with the passing of five decades since those days, my position as a mere minion remains unchanged. Having acquired some 'life perspective' from him(father) – just as a matter of course – at least I acquired something in this regard, in stark contrast to most other people that I have befriended, associated with or fought, since I was a boy, through a span of more than fifty years. Nearly all of these have mimicked – with disturbing clarity and vividness - state representatives who have controlled and who have manipulated the state propaganda mechanism – the media, the

BBC/ITV and the press etc – through the post WW2 decades. All of them, because their parents have been perpetually daunted with the complexity of the world political arena, with George Orwell aghast, have accepted – without much resistance – the simplistic contentions of 'the state'. The story is of old. Their families didn't go there because they were too busy scratching an existence in the midst of the 'competitive gains' world. Characteristically, they naturally adopt their parent's approach, hoping to gain more. Really, they have no political views of worth. With this atmosphere prevailing, 'the state' continues with its free run. The state is administered by 'the establishment' which functions in opposition to 'merit' and 'equity' in support of nepotism and/or patronage. Taking just a few mortals standing in the shadow of the lower league, it elevates them into the opposing realm of grandeur, just to revitalise the false conception that all underlings can potentially succeed through hard work, innovation, bravery, effort, and more particularly lately, greed or sensationalism. The truth is however, that most of those bathed in the grandeur twilight have never actually been forced to remove grime and grit from underneath their finger nails. More pertinently, many have never washed their own clothes, and most have never – ever – had to consider the price of a loaf of bread or a bottle of milk. Just pawns in the grand chess game, the disciples of the establishment point to them saying: "Look, we aren't elite. We encourage and promote your kind, all of the time."

Make no mistake about it, since William the Conqueror arrived here, there has always been the establishment's 'network' – an intricately contrived one at that – of favour and patronage, comprising usually of 'the old boy network' and 'the old school tie brigade' which subjectively function on the basis of opinion and gratification, in total opposition to objectivity, merit and equity. With the monarchy at the pinnacle of it all – as it always has been in this country – the Queen's military, the Queen's judiciary/courts, the police, the whole of the civil service, the NHS, all private and state schools and many civil non-profit organisations operate on the basis of patronage and/or favour. The source of individual success in Britain – now, as always before – is all to do with who you know, not what you know. This means inevitably that many individuals – who are deemed capable and successful – should not actually be doing what they are doing, because a very large number of more suitable people have – by the implication of their non-fraternising personalities and their social class – been excluded from the success arena. Worse, a number of those enjoying authority within the current 'corrupt' framework of national control, have been able to pursue – callously and cruelly - their own personal interests, often to the detriment of many of those dependent on their integrity and empathy. Within the image of the contemporary public scene – with all of its anomalies – many people in Britain now, know the true worth of these comments. Having trusted the Disreali and the Churchill types through the centuries – even the Blair types – to the point of sacrificing their lives and jeopardising their families, why do they now exhibit rebellious tendencies that currently threaten the very foundations of Britain's age old social framework? Because of new technology and what it has brought to us all. Because of the 'Counter-Network' that has recently evolved as a consequence.

Section Two:
The Prime Phobia Of Establishments – Rebellion:

With the continuation of coercion by their monarchs - and with the adamance of ecclesiastic conformity exponents - for centuries, the British people – the ordinary folk – for the first time ever in the year 1819 AD, gathered in a large mass of numbers – 60,000 – at St Peter's Field, Manchester to protest about their poverty. Then occurred, what has been identified since as the 'Peterloo Massacre'. Very typically – in accordance with tradition – they were attacked by cavalry officers, swiping sabres at them and by soldiers shooting to kill. All typified the way things in Britain had always been, until that day. After this occasion however, the majority of the 'underlings' refused to be cajoled any more. Violent force and cruel retribution – the fundamental tools of the traditional establishment – became redundant, due to the French revolutionary scenario, which then, was still fresh in the minds of all Europeans. This clearly demonstrated the potential consequences of forced rule through violent coercion. After Peterloo, the tide of rebellion in Britain could only be stemmed by winning hearts and minds – as it is so often inaptly put nowadays - within the framework of a new preliminary democracy. All of which meant that the ordinary people of Britain – the people that toiled and sweated in the mines and in the factories - had to be hoaxed into disbelieving those with rebellious contentions. Thus evolved the new 'control expedient' of perpetual hoodwinking, with every limb of the establishment in action. Perpetual because 'whistleblowers' – to be suppressed and muted at any cost – have appeared – and are still appearing – more and more frequently with the passing of each and every decade. All of which nowadays, extends far into the international contemporary scene. Controversial names such as Julian Assage and Edward Snowdon are notorious now. Poor old Bradley Manning.

Nationally, because the establishment's prerogative always was – and still is - to shape the nation and all of its tributaries: the 'national celebration' agenda – always heavily 'monarchy' weighted – and the national sports agenda, have always – and will always – be construed to appear noble, even elitist. More particularly, 'of old', such agendas have always paved the way for massive congregations of people to idolise – and to worship, in the broadest sense – particular persons, who, through their heritage, their allegiances and/or their efforts, are representative of the prevailing 'state' identity, thus desired and pursued by the establishment. From early modern times, printed media – duly influencing and often opposing lots and lots of 'grapevines' – has been controlled by the establishment, on occasions – especially during war times – directly and extremely. During the 1960s – which was the heyday of 'newspaper' media – Prime Minister Harold Wilson busied himself quite typically with the successive issue of 'D' notices to prevent the tarnishment of the state image. Such action was not precedent then, it was – and still is – custom 'of-old', invoked most often behind the masque of state security protection. In this context, the meaning of the renowned Beaverbook/Churchill affiliation is not to be disregarded in our history literature, or indeed, within any other media. It reveals the real truth to discernible people. Beaverbrook was Churchill's puppet, vigorously broadcasting all of his dictums, just as much as 'Lord Haw-Haw' broadcasted for Hitler during

WW2. Now however, with the advent and with the enormous ascendancy of radio, television and the computing 'Internet' wonderland, all has changed, has it not? Only China and North Korea have managed to asphyxiate the Internet to date. The fearful question is: Will the current British 'Establishment' get to be able to control this also, in the future?

Section Three:
When Organised Tyranny Began In England:

For the English, the Welsh and eventually for the Scots – the implications of '1066 and all of that' were profound. The true identities of individuals were annihilated. They were forfeited, never to be restored. Later though, Geoffrey Chaucer – along with a few his contemporaries – liberated the English language from the shackles of restricted colloquialism, deliberately circumvented by the Normans. A cunning salvation in reality, 'Canterbury Tales'(Geoffrey Chaucer) was beyond diminution. From 1066 until the Chaucer era, only French literature – in an official form – existed in England. Possible only because most of the Norman oppressors and all of the incumbent English, were unable to read anyway. Not that this mattered much. England was not administered in those days with formal dictate scripts, to be adhered to. The price to be paid for rebellion against the directives of the barons, was death, by the sword or by the rope, or even worse, by gut wrenching. All was demonstrated, word mongered and grapevined with the extensive mobility of horse mounted knights, marauding everywhere. For those that were slow 'to get the message', even the new art of the day – Norman inspired, and Norman extolled art – told stories and sequenced events, often in tapestry form – instead of just producing sketched or painted facsimiles. In this way – visually – the threat of dastardly prosecution was communicated to the illiterate and the ignorant; all abound.

The conqueror's knights enslaved their minions unsentimentally to obtain manpower, to build defensive wooden stockades, and then – to consolidate – stone constructed castles which were strategically placed to facilitate broad based oppression. White Castle – just within the English boundary nowadays – is a day's horse ride from Caerphilly Castle, Grosmont Castle is a day's horse ride from White Castle, Skenfrith Castle is a day's horse ride from Grosmont Castle, and Raglan Castle is also a day's horse ride from Skenfrith Castle, and so on. The great Welsh leader 'Llewellyn the Great' may have marauded about his land freely, but he was unable to eliminate his enemies, due to the existence of these fortifications, reinforced and augmented by Henry II. The terrorising force of the early Norman invasion – evolving into the Plantagenet era - was sustained well beyond Llewellyn's prevalence, encroaching, oppressing and most of the time, terrifying the incumbent population of England and Wales. Particularly, all was extended with 'Serfs' enslaved to 'Villains' for the production of agricultural produce, always usurped for the benefit of the 'Noble' class. Where the Roman Empire was formed and sustained on the basis of conquer and enslave, medieval England – within the magnificent network of stone fortified castles – reverted yet again into the depths of Roman styled Armageddon. Starkly, for all native incumbents, upward social mobility from the oppressed to the oppressors was a utopian aspiration, impossible under any circumstances. Particularly this was due to the chain of patronage, ingrained within the Norman/Plantagenet military styled culture which communicated with the use of an alien language; French, retaining elitism considerably. Elevation into the ecclesiastic fold was also impossible at local level, with the Pope in Rome strictly overseeing each and all of his agents, in all of the churches and the monasteries, most of whom communicated by means of the old Roman Latin language, which of course was a strong feature of the 'Holy Roman Empire'. By the year 1215 AD, with the creation of Magna-Carta, all of the minions of England and Wales were doomed to remain as underlings – serfs enslaved to barons – because all of the protective provisions of Magna-Carta applied only to 'free men', then, synonymously property owners of some sort. This is the way it remained in reality – for over seven hundred years, believe it or not – until the first 'Representation of the Peoples Act' arrived in the year 1928 AD.

Section Four:
Regency-Papacy Unions:

In the meantime, the regency/papacy conspiracy that prevailed in England between king John 1st and Pope Innocent 3rd in Avignon then, is confirmed emphatically with John's reaction to Magna Carta. Produced by an ecclesiastic agent of his barons – and subsequently written in Latin – John – being confused about its authenticity – took it to the Pope to be reviewed. In keeping with his conceived authority, bolstered by the Pope, it was subsequently rebuked. Truly, John and the Pope were in cahoots with each other, and so were all of the other regents throughout the lands of Europe 'to-be', all co-existing within the realms of the 'Holy Roman Empire'. In reality, the green and pleasant land of England – partially protected by the seas that surrounded it – after 1066 and all of that, became enmeshed with the prevailing tyrannical realms of its nearest neighbours on the European land mass. Stretching from the Atlantic coast at Bretagne and Aquitaine all the way across to Ottoman territory, multitudes of provinces vehemently ruled by princes and kings – at the 1066 juncture, and beyond – expanded and contracted – and frequently disappeared altogether – through the ages, due to the 'land' and the 'power' lust of many of the incumbent monarchs, virtually all adopting the principle of hereditary control over their humble subjects. All perpetually kept humble by force, fear and bludgeonry, synonymous with the revered, the immortalised and the unencroachable knights – such as 'The Order Of The Garter' incumbents - of the royal realms. Thus, all of the minions – those not directly receiving the patronage of their monarchs - of the land mass that is known now as Europe, being continuously oppressed, have been – and still remain – obedient and subservient in the face of monarchically construed customs of old, designed and imposed principally, to control them. This phenomenon is a vivid reality, only now being challenged – with the aid of contemporary technology, and particularly within the scene of the Internet – by the populations of ancient lands in the middle east of the world, who were similarly tyrannised through numerous millennia, but who now find themselves oppressed – and in Syria even subjugated – by sultans, amires and pseudo-kings and pseudo presidents of the 'Hassan' kind. Knowing that Europeans – and Americans of course – typically enjoy more freedom, and possess more than they do, their aspirational agitations have taken them into Armageddon, the extent of which remains indeterminable to this day.

Ironically, the free world that they think exists to their west, is actually an unreal Utopia. For all that has occurred since '*Charlemagne', the old serfs of Europe are still serfs. They have elevated themselves up the developmental ladder further, but they are most definitely still serfs. Born of ignorance, even if it is a little less than that of their eastern counterparts.

*Charlemagne: King Charles 5th, also crowned as the Emperor of the '*Holy Roman Emperor' in the year 800 AD.

You see, unlike my father, none of them have ever managed to see a way through the smoke and the mirrors that have always been evident in the midst of all of the European turmoil since 'Charlemagne'. Really, since the dark ages that persisted after the fall of the Roman Empire. Long ago indeed. In this context a new renaissance is well overdue. Just like Stalin, my father would hold no truck with church people, whether orthodox or unusual, conventional or revolutionary, because their motives always were – and still are – clandestine in the context of politics and power. Secretive conspirators cloaked in hypocrisy and often possessed with dubious intent. For all of his neglect of me, and for all of his eventual detriment towards me, he granted me as a child an extremely valuable salvation. He respected my prerogative to decide upon my own interests in relation to the so called spiritual religious world. More so, he supported me whenever I chose to resist the affronts of outward influences in this regard. In the midst of schooling establishments, he fended all away from me and left me to choose for myself, without attempting to influence me in his interests. Ironically in the midst of all of this, the state – the newly styled legislative state –

came to assist me also with a shield, in the form of the 1948 education act of Parliament.

Only because of this approach in my upbringing, is it possible now to identify – with a totally impartial perspective – the true 'bigamist' of Europe through the ages, that appeased all of the despotic princes and kings while pretending to empathise with each and all of its lowly subjects, whether individuals, or communities. Multitudes of lowly minions – of the serf kind – accepted contentions that all of the princes and the kings were noble – spiritually good people – to be revered, respected, and most particularly, to be followed in their quest to embattle, to suffer and to 'die' for the cause of 'God'. Truly, the principal conspirer of the monarchical suppression of all of the minions within all of the realms was the strong Christian religious forum – later to form the 'Holy Roman Empire' - gathered ubiquitously in Avignon in the Abbey of Saint-Ruf from the year 1309 AD to the year 1377AD. Subsequent to Charlemagne being crowned as the emperor of this – restored Roman – empire, all of the beings in Europe were told that all of the squeaky-clean fraternity – the Christian clerics, who were exclusively educated and knowledgeable – trusted one of the despotic monarchs enough to revere him as their symbolic leader. Conversely, as long as he – and all of the others like him – provided licence to the Avignon 'papacy', they were supported and secured; most certainly not opposed in their control of the minions, needed to grow/generate their riches and to extend their powers. Ostensibly then, the control strategy of all of the minions shifted from pure tyranny all of the time, to proportions of tyranny, combined with morality idolism – the Ten Commandments and all of that – and monarchy idolism. In the midst of it all, the deprivation of critical information was not deliberately imposed, but it was universally apparent because of the absence of literacy which remained entrenched exclusively in the ecclesiastic void.

'Holy Roman Empire'
Wikipeadia Extract:

In a famous assessment of the name, the French Enlightenment writer Voltaire remarked sardonically: "This agglomeration which was called and which still calls itself the Holy Roman Empire was neither holy, nor Roman, nor an empire."

The precise term Holy Roman Empire was not used until the 13th century, but the concept of translatio imperii ("transfer of rule") was fundamental to the prestige of the emperor, the notion that he held supreme power inherited from the emperors of Rome. The office of Holy Roman Emperor was traditionally elective, although frequently controlled by dynasties. The German prince-electors, the highest ranking noblemen of the empire, usually elected one of their peers as "King of the Romans", and he would later be crowned emperor by the Pope; the tradition of papal coronations was discontinued in the 16th century. The empire never achieved the extent of political unification formed in France, evolving instead into a decentralised, limited elective monarchy composed of hundreds of sub-units, principalities, duchies, counties, Free Imperial Cities, and other domains. The power of the emperor was limited, and while the various princes, lords, and kings of the empire were vassals and subjects who owed the emperor their allegiance, they also possessed an extent of privileges that gave them de-facto sovereignty within their territories. Emperor Francis II dissolved the empire on August 6, 1806, after its defeat by Napoleon at the Battle of Austerlitz

End Of The First Section: Wikipeadia Extract – Holy Roman Empire

Within the structure of this 'Papacy/Monarchs pact', tyranny – of old – was retained in a somewhat refined form, purporting the new concept of 'justice'. Subjects of crowns contravening either papal or royal protocols were newly provided a voice in community gatherings, formed of 'jurors', where penal actions were determined. The real context from old remained unchanged for many centuries however. The Papacy and the monarchs prosecuted any sort of rebuttal to their authority with vehemence. Where jurors unwittingly participated in this prosecution, they were most often tyrannical accomplices. They were left without influence on penalties, which frequently evolved into death ceremonies held in the midst of townships, culminating into body suspensions over the raging infernoes of bonfires. The fate of Joan of Arch and a favourite expedient of 'Witchfinder Generals' up to and including Cromwellian times in England. Congruently, monarchy and morality idolism reinforced absolute subservience to God, to Christ and to the reigning monarch. Demonstrated most explicitly by prayers, by all sorts of other public moan and groan gestures and by all sorts of ceremonies, for marriage, for funerals, for coronations, for consecrations and remembrances: all of a Christian religious basis. Truly, monarchical styled European dominions – forever wrangling in their midst – remained entwined in the Papacy network for a very long time indeed. Until the long succession of crusade wars – in opposition to the Muslim empires - were lost, and even beyond. In fact, until Napoleon Bonaparte appeared on the European scene in force.

From Charlemagne through to Napoleon Bonaparte in time terms, a remarkable surge of the fusion of communities, monarchies, regencies and states occurred. Because so many existed at the start of it all, integration and consolidation were inevitable in terms of evolutionary progress. Not an easy form of progress though, and particularly, not a simple one either. While still remaining subordinate to the emperor of the 'Holy Roman Empire', the princes of the old Germanies still involved themselves with all kinds of rivalry. Contrastingly, numerous Franka regencies in western Europe, slowly but surely through four to five centuries – with the help of some magnificent defensive infrastructure – fused into the nation of France, ruled by a single monarch by 1584 AD. Long before this event however, the Danish invaders of the East Anglian coast of England were still the devils of adversity for William the Conqueror's regency descendants, just as much as they had been for their Anglo-Saxon predecessors, Harold 2nd, and Alfred the Great, before him. Yet truly, England became integrated – not quite on a par with France – subtely, with the marriage union of Henry 7th and Elizabeth of York in the year 1485 AD, in the immediate wake of the battle of Bosworth Field. Here, Henry quelled the forces of the king of the shires of York, Richard 3rd, but this significant military success facilitated oppression, not union. Rather, England became solidly homogenous by means of the subsequent marriage, which invoked true fusion between the red and the white rose regencies. Yet, Scotland and Ireland continued to exist outwardly.

'Holy Roman Empire'
Wikipeadia Extracts:

1122 Concordat of Worms – Henry V:
Kings often employed bishops in administrative affairs and often determined who would be appointed to ecclesiastical offices. In the wake of the Cluniac Reforms, this involvement was increasingly seen as inappropriate by the Papacy. The reform Pope Gregory 7th was determined to oppose such practices, leading to the Investiture Controversy with King Henry 4th 1056–1106 who repudiated the Pope's interference and persuaded his bishops to excommunicate the Pope, whom he famously addressed by his born name "Hildebrand", rather than his regnal name "Pope Gregory 7th". The Pope, in turn, excommunicated the king, declared him deposed, and dissolved the oaths of loyalty made to Henry. The king found himself with almost no political support and was forced to make the famous Walk to Canossa in 1077.

Rise of the territories after the Hohenstaufen:
The difficulties in electing the king eventually led to the emergence of a fixed college of Prince-electors, whose composition and procedures were set forth in the Golden Bull of 1356, which was valid until 1806. This development probably best symbolises the emerging duality between emperor and realm (Kaiser und Reich), which were no longer considered identical. The Golden Bull also set the election system of the Holy Roman Emperor. The emperor now had to be elected by a majority rather than by consent of all seven electors. For electors the title became hereditary, and they were given the right to mint coins and to exercise jurisdiction. Also their sons were to know

the imperial languages – German, Italian, and Czech.

End Of The Second Section: Wikipeadia Extract – Holy Roman Empire

Section Five:
The 'Order Of The Garter' Prevails:

Even in the fury and the perils of WW2, has the United Kingdom ever been completely unified? My father – being quite a bright boy – found himself fully engaged as an aviator in the Royal Air Force, when it was fighting Hitler. Quite a conflict in his mind, being conscripted and being an ardent anti-royalist. Why should officers – who he closely worked with – eat in their mess with silver cutlery and with waiters abound, when he had to obtain his food by standing in a long queue with a slop bowl outstretched, virtually like a prison inmate? All faced combat with the same dangers. The answer was of course, that the establishment really preferred royalists – the upper classes – but there weren't enough of them. He was temporarily 'included' into the fold, but not with full sanction, and of course, he had to return to his lowly position when it was all over.

Profoundly, at the juncture of the year 1944 AD – in accordance with my father's experiences - the 'Order of the Garter' regime style, persisted in the 'United Kingdom', which for all of its facades, had not been – and still is not – really united. In fact nowadays, all will agree that it is conspicuously fragmenting. Consistently – and I mean very consistently – the establishment in Britain – and traditionally in the rest of Europe – has exhibited ridiculous levels of determination born of paranoia to retain 'control' and to perpetuate its particular brand of ideology. The latter was seriously dented by the demise of Louis 16th's, which in turn, elevated Napoleon Bonaparte, with all of the ramifications of military empires. Yet, all of it had occurred previously in Britain had it not? During the reign of Charles 1st, with Oliver Cromwell evolving eventually as a new type of monarch. In short, the English and the French attempts to establish constitutional democracy were not at all successful, although at least the French did manage – eventually - to permanently extinguish the last of the Bourbons. None of this turned out to be quite suitable for the likes of Danton, Paine, Voltaire or Ruesso, however.

By the year 1819 – the year of the Peterloo Tory massacre of lowly minions in Britain – the writing was on the wall, clearly and precisely. Total control of the masses in England at least by means of violent subversion became newly precarious – even dangerous - due to 'word of mouth' communications about events occurring in other parts of the world. This 'grapevine' broadcasted the real potential of people unification to overthrow establishments. From this time, the aristocracy – synonymous with land ownership – and the derelict remnants of 'The Holy Roman Empire' – realised that violent repression was redundant, as the principal strategy of people suppression. The parliamentary government of the day was really nothing to do with it all, because due to the ridiculous privileges granted to land owners and the new factory capitalists, it was merely a perpetual puppet show, mimicking the desires of the church and the gentry, considering of course, that the church in England – and Wales and Scotland – was at that time, and still is – a major land owner.

Section Six:
Pioneering Public Control Tactics In Britain:

'Holy Roman Empire'
Wikipeadia Extract:

The Seven Prince-electors prospective Emperor had first to be elected King of the Romans. German kings had been elected since the 9th century; at that point they were chosen by the leaders of the five most important tribes (the Salian Franks of Lorraine, Ripuarian Franks of Franconia, Saxons, Bavarians and Swabians). In the Holy Roman Empire, the main dukes and bishops of the kingdom elected the King of the Romans. In 1356, Emperor Charles 4th issued the Golden Bull, which limited the electors to seven: the King of Bohemia, the Count Palatine of the Rhine, the Duke of Saxony, the Margrave of Brandenburg and the archbishops of Cologne, Mainz, and Trier. During the Thirty Years' War, the Duke of Bavaria was given the right to vote as the eighth elector. A candidate for election would be expected to offer concessions of land or money to the electors in order to secure their vote.

After being elected, the King of the Romans could theoretically claim the title of "Emperor" only after being crowned by the Pope. In many cases, this took several years while the King was held up by other tasks: frequently he first had to resolve conflicts in rebellious northern Italy, or was in quarrel with the Pope himself. Later Emperors dispensed with the papal coronation altogether, being content with the styling Emperor-Elect: the last Emperor to be crowned by the Pope was Charles V in 1530.

End Of The Third Section: Wikipeadia Extract – Holy Roman Empire

Yet the introduction of universal adult suffrage – votes for all and sundry; a say in the affairs of the nation – was never a true intent then, or since. The way out of wrangles like Peterloo was to glorify and to inflate the value of pitifully insignificant votes to suitable 'subjects of the crown' which by the year 1832 AD, certainly did not include women or non-owners of property. Constitutional reforms were introduced in this year, after being vigorously resisted by the grand 'Duke of Wellington' during his time as Prime Minister of Britain between the years 1828-1830 AD. They did not alter the constitutional structure of Britain, by one iota; they just changed the mass's – the minion's - conception of it. In their ignorance, who could blame their acceptance of the new pseudo concept of democracy? Especially because all of the other minions of the world still existed in the midst of tyranny. Then, the whole entity of the British nation – it appeared to most – needed to retain its stance, its structure and most particularly its ambitions, just to survive and to prosper in a world of increasing hostility. During the Naopoleonic wars, personal interests were most certainly subordinate to the conquest of Napoleon Bonaparte. Similarly, Elizabeth Ist's subjects had subordinated themselves during the period when Philip 2nd of Spain was prominent and powerful. Both of these international facades forced the hungry British populace – deprived of foreign food imports – to enclose agricultural land for frequent crop rotations, to control food variety and to increase food outputs. Characteristically, the British nation adapted and innovated, like it had during previous eras, and as it would do in the future, on numerous occasions.

Duly, the forfeiture of 'violent oppression' control methods – due to the French revolution - inspired a newly found theme of localised direct control, with new police forces, resourced to increased levels of sophistication. 'Bobbies' – created by Robert Peel(Home Secretary in the year 1822 AD) – also known as 'Peelers' were born, initially to uphold all of the virtues of the Anglican church in England and Ireland. 'Peelers' were associated with oranges, which in turn were associated with king William of Orange, by implication and by legacy, a notable suppressor of Catholicism. In the event, 'Bobbies' became law enforcers at local level - in preference to the engagement of conveniently placed military contingencies - who were always seen as frightful 'armed belligerents'. In this context, 'Bobbies' were not – and still are not – armed. In contrast to the military, based in new police stations, they evolved as integrated elements of local societies, better situated to detect and prevent breaches of the prevailing laws of their time. However, since their inception, difficulties have persisted in relation to the prosecution of 'criminals within - with the prosecution of 'Bobbies' that break the law – in the midst of 'closed Police shops', just as sheep flock together in times of crisis. In a complementary fashion, the 'King's' courts – manned mostly by the 'Old School Tie' brigades that held the King's favour – duly enforced the old common law - devised by the original Norman barons - with increased proliferation, but not commonly with comparative sophistication. With vehemence – as always beforehand – the judiciary of Great Britain – which comprised, and still comprises a core element of the establishment – enforced the 'old order' of things steadfastly and resiliently. No force in the land – even 'People Power' – could change this phenomenon. Quite definitely, it remains unchanged to this day, even with the frequent introduction of numerous statutes that have restricted the interpretive powers of judges against common law bias. In fact, one 'man' one vote every-so-often – established somewhat precariously in 1832 – did not even dent this armour-clad order. The evidence of this conclusion lies in the appearance of the 'Theft Act 1916', devised principally to prevent all of the deprived minions in the land from acquiring miniscule portions of 'baron' born wealth of old, in a much more sophisticated fashion than previous. Yet, by the time the twentieth century was born, the law of the land emanated from crown subjects, unlike the rest of the European continent. Here – even to this day – the basis of the control of all of its minions originated from the expansion and the entrenchment of the 'Holy Roman Empire'. Roman law in Europe – as opposed to common law in Britain – emanates not from the 'Justinian' elements of the old Byzantine empire, but from the Papacy of Avignon and Rome. Pertinent nowadays, maybe not, because of Napoleonic legacies? Yet, to most anti-church exponents, such origins are pungently poisonous.

'Holy Roman Empire'
Wikipeadia Extract:

Imperial Diet (Holy Roman Empire:
The Imperial Diet was the legislative body of the Holy Roman Empire and theoretically superior to the emperor himself. It was divided into three classes. The first class, the Council of Electors, consisted of the electors, or the princes who could vote for King of the Romans. The second class, the Council of Princes, consisted of the other princes. The Council of Princes was divided into

two "benches," one for secular rulers and one for ecclesiastical ones. Higher-ranking princes had individual votes, while lower-ranking princes were grouped into "colleges" by geography. Each college had one vote. The third class was the Council of Imperial Cities, which was divided into two colleges: Swabia and the Rhine. The Council of Imperial Cities was not fully happy with the others; it could not vote on several matters such as the admission of new territories. The representation of the Free Cities at the Diet had become common since the late Middle Ages. Nevertheless, their participation was formally acknowledged only as late as in 1648 with the Peace of Westphalia ending the Thirty Years' War.

Administrative seats of the emperor:
From 794 – Aachen
1328–1347 – Munich
1355–1437 and 1576-1611 – Prague

End Of The Fourth Section: Wikipeadia Extract – Holy Roman Empire

Section Seven:
Keeping All Of The Minions In Ignorance:

With the 'Papacy' in Rome maintaining a tight grip on all literal communications in the western world – and even the far western world of South America – throughout medieval and the early modern times, the world of all of the minions – throughout Europe, Bohemia and Scandinavia – was dark, and it was kept dark. The power of 'literacy' – the only information source beyond 'grapevines' – was truly monopolised by the Papacy, with its central autocratic control of priests, bishops and archbishops. Paradoxically, with the sacking of all of the monasteries in Britain – and with the removal of all of the Latin bibles in local churches – even this morsel of flickering light was extinguished by Henry 8th. Where most of his populace were unable to read, let alone write – continuously hoping for word-of-mouth enhancements to their lives - the remainder could only guess about the real truth of his conflict with the Pope in Rome. Of all of the importance of communications within any society, in particular, the rules of obedience form the crux of it all, whether simple, or complicated, as they were – and as they still are – with tiering to accommodate different social classes. The most sophisticated documentation with regard to such rule sets is the bible, of old and still, as now. In Henry 8th's day – and during many ages preceding him – those unable to read it depended on its interpreters to convert its contents into verbal nuances, and here lies the plot. The definitive statements within such – through the process of interpretation – were, and still are unrealistically distorted – even forfeited – in the interpreter's favour. To this day, this sort of thing also goes on in courts of law where the basis of governmental legislation is frequently corrupted. Where the judges of courts deliberately misinterpret the true intentions of Parliamentary legislators.

With the remarkable survival of 'Magna Carta - 1215 AD' – with its incorporation of 'Habeas Corpus'(a basis for prosecution must exist) – a realisation inevitably evolves about the intentions of its applicability when it was written. As an archetype rule set, it was only meant to apply to those that were able to read it. Disappointingly, it appears now, to have been applicable only to the lords and the barons of that age; 'free men'. Clearly, with literacy only blessed onto those in control - or those near to the top of the echelons, more usually seeking control – ignorance and illiteracy orchestrated unjust oppression and persecution. Truly the predicament of the minions of England – and everywhere else – then. The bible apart – which through the ages has indoctrinated and directed the 'minions' of the Christian world – written documents of old were created and used by the elite literate to corroborate agreements, to make them binding, usually with the incorporation of a seal and/or a signature, just like the Magna Carta. Other forms of literature – other than the Bible - like Geoffrey Chaucer's 'Canterbury Tales' were very rare. Magnificent artistic efforts in their day. Very prone to disappearance with age, often because the chore of copying them was an extensive and arduous task. Then came the 'Gutenburg*' printing phenomenon by the year 1455 AD, but it took a long time to pick up momentum and gather pace, even with a forceful push-along by 'William Caxton*' during the year 1470s AD. Using the new technology of 'letterpress*' printing to bridge the great void between the English and the French languages, he translated significant French literature into English in print, made possible with 'letterpress'. Breaking the papacy's monopoly of book production, the English language - having been nurtured from its literary birth by Chaucer – began to spread in manageable form in England, but only as far as it could be extended however, in an ignorant world.

All of this happened at least a quarter of a millennium after the Norman invaders of England adapted raw resources to protect themselves. Mining and forging metals into chain mail, into helmets and body armour, and quarrying stone to build formidable defensive castles. Within a century of so later – after nearly all of the incumbents had been subdued - King John 1st then found the need to lay siege to many of the stone fortresses built by his forefathers, to quash widespread 'baron' rebellions. A bit of a nuisance for him, of his own father's making in an ironic sort of way. Where within the dominions of the future France, power consolidation evolved with the intermarriage of the monarchs – combining regencies – and by inter-regency wars, within the Germanies of Franka and Gothic descent, Frederick Barbarossa the Red Beard, Duke of Swabia, King of Germany and eventually, Emperor of the Holy Roman Empire, extended his regency over the Alps into what is now, northern Italy as far as Rome. Unlike the Angevin kings of Britain, the Papacy and all in the Germanies were from the start of it all in 800 AD, always closely entwined with the Papacy, really as one, with popes overseeing spiritualism and with monarchs supporting and beholding them, as forceful, wealthy and powerful overseers of their realms. All formed the 'Holy Roman Empire', within which boundaries flexed like the tides of the world's oceans in accordance with particular Papacy/Regency alliances. In all, a lot of continuous 'Christian' war mongering all over the land that was eventually recognised as Europe. As if local ambitions weren't enough, where a lot of inter-sultanic 'Muslim' war mongering was also occurring all over the land that was eventually recognised as Arabia, many Christian monarchs including Richard 1st – the Lionheart – in Frederick's shadow, campaigned against Saladin to claim Jerusalem for Christianity. Where Frederick Red Beard perished in this endeavour, the Lionheart survived. Like many of his contemporaries on the continental land mass, he continued to be wholly engaged in the establishment of territorial sovereignty, particularly within the Normandy and the Aquataine regions of France, which he died defending in 1199AD.

'Holy Roman Empire'
Wikipeadia Extract:

The shift in power away from the emperor is also revealed in the way the post-Hohenstaufen kings attempted to sustain their power. Earlier, the Empire's strength (and finances) greatly relied on the Empire's own lands, the so-called Reichsgut, which always belonged to the king of the day and included many Imperial Cities. After the 13th century, the relevance of the Reichsgut faded, even though some parts of it remained until the Empire's end in 1806. Instead, the Reichsgut was increasingly pawned to local dukes, sometimes to raise money for the Empire, but more frequently to reward faithful duty or as an attempt to establish control over the dukes. The direct governance of the Reichsgut no longer matched the needs of either the king or the dukes.

At the Battle of Vienna (1683), the Army of the Holy Roman Empire, led by the Polish King John 3rd Sobieski, decisively defeated a large Turkish army, ending the western colonial Ottoman advance and leading to the eventual dismemberment of the Ottoman Empire in Europe. The HRE army was half Polish/Lithuanian Commonwealth forces, mostly cavalry, and half Holy Roman Empire forces (German/Austrian), mostly infantry.

The actual end of the empire came in several steps. The Peace of Westphalia in 1648, which ended the Thirty Years' War, gave the territories almost complete sovereignty. The Swiss Confederation, which had already established quasi-independence in 1499, as well as the Northern Netherlands, left the Empire. The Habsburg Emperors focused on consolidating their own estates in Austria and elsewhere.

The Empire was formally dissolved on August 6, 1806, when the last Holy Roman Emperor Francis 2nd (from 1804, Emperor Francis I of Austria) abdicated, following a military defeat by the French under Napoleon at Austerlitz. Napoleon reorganised much of the Empire into the Confederation of the Rhine, a French satellite. Francis' House of Habsburg-Lorraine survived the demise of the Empire, continuing to reign as Emperors of Austria and Kings of Hungary until the Habsburg empire's final dissolution in 1918 in the aftermath of World War I.

End Of The Fifth Section: Wikipeadia Extract – Holy Roman Empire

Section Eight:
Malignant Catholicism – On The Back Of Empire Builders:

In the meantime, the Papacy - with thwarted ambitions in the east – easily spread its tentacles with force and with solidity over the west of the continental land mass. After establishing Aragon in the face of the Moors, the Holy Roman Empire extended vastly to the south and to the west – mostly through Crusader support and bloody combat – eventually to spread Catholicism within the bounds of all of the lands meeting the Mediterranean sea and the Atlantic ocean, bordering France in the north. In the modern context, these are now the lands of Portugal and Spain. By the end of this westward surge, all of the Moors were duly banished back to north Africa by the year 1492 AD. These events were profound to the point of being perhaps, the pinnacles of world history. They paved the way for long standing inter-nobility marriage conventions to be applied in this part of Europe. 'Alfonso', 'Sancho' and 'Manuel' dynasties evolved, paving the way, not only for the creation of the nation state of Portugal, but also for the spread of Catholicism over the Atlantic ocean westwards, towards the south American continent. Augmenting the great seafaring traditions of Christopher Columbus and Vasco De Gama, the Papacy in Rome, through Portuguese – and subsequent Spanish – adventurism, gained valuable opportunities to breath the wrath of religious indoctrination throughout the South American continent, initially smothering Brazil. Also – very ominously – in direct connection to these events, the world's first incident of slavery trading occurred, and it continued unabated by the Papacy or any of its regencies, for many centuries. The prime regency of future Europe – Hapsburg – significantly augmented early Portuguese ventures – through Maxmillian 1st and Charles 5th – after it consolidated its power in Austria, the Nederland, Italy and Spain with devastating continuity, especially in Spain. Charles 5th's Spanish regency, subsequently included Peru, all of which was inherited by his son, Philip 1st, who was also Philip 2nd of the Hapsburg dynasty. Then Philip 1st – with the engulfment of Portugal by Spain – ascended as the sovereign of Portugal, but also as the overseer of Portugal's Brazilian slave colony. All amounted to a lot of the world beyond the Atlantic ocean. With the Papacy intricately entwined with the Hapsburg dynasty, this meant that the significant civilisations of old in the whole of the South American continent had to be obliterated in the name of Catholicism. All occurred for God and 'gold'.

Much more recently, my mother - a widow with three children and a daughter of a Jehovah's Witness matriarch - was lobotomised by the establishment of the British state when I was aged five years. Then she was incarcerated in a mental institution for fifteen years contiguously. Because some of her faculties had been destroyed, and because she had been institutionalised for such a long time, she failed to cope after being placed back into society. She was returned to a mental hospital and remained in it until she died twenty five years or so later. My young father who married my mother(a widow) did so under the guise of an anti-war campaigner – with two of his brother-in-laws imprisoned as conscientious objectors – and with the acceptance of the doctrines of Jehovah's Witnesses, but afterwards returned to the roots of his atheist upbringing, re-adopting atheism. Dependently, my mother – and all of her children, including myself – was forced to follow, to a location beyond the tentacles of her relatives. With the faith of her parents – and her faith – abandoned and with her children violently assaulted day by day – supposedly in the cause of some sort of manic puritanism – she descended – inevitably and distinctively – into the realms of terror. Irrevocably so with the breach of her trust, on discovering that her new tyrannical husband was also an adulterer. Meanwhile, her husband(my father, a Judah and an ardent disciple of Satan) remained steadfastly on the bandwagon of anti-war and anti-weapons.

Section Nine:
Weapons And Palaces:

The manic Norman inclination to suppress, to control and to terrorise its subverted populace in England and in Wales was characteristically the way of life all about the regencies of the European land mass 'to-be', extended very much into the east of Bohemia in the days of Frederick Barbarossa. Two centuries or so later, England's Angevin dynasties of Henry 1st and Henry 2nd raged with remarkable military prowess through Normandy. By this time, the conquering and the control of valuable territories – and all of the minions within them – was not just about knights brandishing swords all about the place. It was also about besieging - and sometimes demolishing - encountered fortresses that protected opposing armies. Outcomes were not always certain when horses, swords and spikes faced solid granite walls that could spit out boiling oil. Nor were they, in the face of equally equipped armies. What came then, was not the diminishment of the will of the oppressors, but weapons 'innovation', to gain advantage. Just as 'trebuchets' successfully terrorised the inmates of medieval castles all about western regencies, long-bow archers – when precisely organised en-mass – nullified absolutely, the power of knights brandishing swords. The long-bow weapons were of old, but they could form a single – massive – affronting weapon when combined and used simultaneously, especially when they were placed cleverly, in the midst of battle scenes. In this context, Winston Churchill's two fingered gesture during WW2 is ominous and distinct. This gesture is symbolic of English long-bow archers, of the kind that relished in their victory at Agincourt. Since then – most affirmably – the British have been – and still are – prominent pioneers of war weapons innovation, on a par with France and second only to the United States of America. France's prowess in this regard was clearly demonstrated during the Falklands war, with the chilling realisations of the British navy, when faced with Exocet missile jeopardy. Also, France still retains an independent nuclear capability.

The British pre-occupation with the development and the production of war weapons is truly a fascinating facet, because it 'connects' with the 'Holy Roman Empire', and particularly with the Hapsburg dynasty. Henry 8th was the first monarch of the western dominions to seek exclusion from Catholicism. Most historians to this day have consistently contended that Henry sacked the catholic monasteries in England and Wales in order to remove the Pope from his personal affairs. My contention is that this view is idiosyncratic, not particularly appreciative of the world that prevailed during his time. As we all truly know now, Philip 1st of Spain – Philip 2nd of Hapsburg – descended into the depths of iniquity, enmeshed, entwined and inextricably collusive with the 'Holy Roman Empire' at the peak of its ascendancy in the world. Over-awed with its own importance, for at least five centuries – actually eight, from the time of Charlemagne – it had conspired with all of the monarchs of all of the catholic regencies throughout the European continent to glorify God, which was actually all about glorifying it, the Pope and the Hapsburgs. It had successfully hoodwinked all of the minions in all of the regencies to involve themselves with the building of 'gold plated' – no expense spared – palaces within every niche of every society/community. Astonishingly nowadays, few see churches and cathedrals in this form, most probably because this sort of architecture was already all about, at their birth. All is a weird fixation, totally devoid of any sort of logic: "Churches must exist – as they always have - to enable me to worship God". As to why they should be filled – universally – with all sorts of paraphinalia, rarely invokes a response from such exponents, however. Incorporating the finest art of the most elite artists in the land, of that era – and all subsequent eras - everywhere, with fantastically adorned stained glass windows, lead lined and often grasping the enhancement of the daily Sun. Populated with bishops and archbishops wearing ludicrous garments of glory. Gold alters, arrays of gold candlesticks, long red carpets, and oak-clad or cloistered internal roofing. Lead lined external roofing, double clad usually, with the best slate tiles available. All standing dominant and perpetual, while the minions grovelled for morsels of food from day to day, and boded in derelict dens. All just because the scope of vision for most minions was no greater than there own dominion, and most emphatically because they could not read. In seeking salvation, they had always to rely on verbal advice – gestures and ceremonies full of gestures - from the Papacy, all of the time while it was conspiring with their subversive rulers.

In the case of Charles 5th and Philip 2nd of Spain – successive Hapsburg heirs – who were Henry 8th's arch enemies, Spanish rule descended down the slippery slope of a corrupt hegemony, initiated by Charles 5th's 'Conquistadores' of the likes of Hernan Cortes who annihilated the Aztec civilisation in the region of Mexico. Likewise, the Spanish colonialist Francisco Pizzaro who sacked and murdered the Inca civilisation in Peru, and Diego de Almagro, who extended all of the bludgeoning into Chile. All for God supposedly, but more particularly for 'gold', to be shipped back to Spain, with simplistic notions about how all of the gentry at home would become extraordinarily wealthy. With the assistance of very few men, Pizzaro succeeded due to Spain's maritime inheritance from Portugal, extolling unequalled seafaring and navigation prowess, but also due – significantly – to advancements in the technology of war weapons. When he was most active, 'canons' were used pioneeringly in battles to quell Cuba(1511) and the land of the Incas(1519). In the wake of South American conquests, immense tonnages of gold and silver were shipped to Spain by means of Charles 5th's new expanded navy – consolidated by Philip 2nd - which eventually ruled the Atlantic in the south and in the north within the bounds of Britain and Ireland. The value of sea power with the use of canon-armed ocean sailing ships was realised by Henry 8th who invested in an opposing navy, not altogether successfully. His flagship Mary Rose met her grief in the English Solent, we all know, due to prevailing infant knowledge of fighting wars in this way.

Section Ten:
Henry 8th In The Face Of The Founder Of Propaganda

Really, Henry 8th of England was belligerent in the face of the new 'all powerful' Spanish navy because the safe passage of ships bound for his kingdom were seriously threatened and hindered. Additionally, he was heretic of the 'Holy Roman Empire' because of his personal matrimonial circumstances, which to date, have received substantial attention from historians, and which – because they have been considered out of context – have amounted to a lot of narrow minded 'domestic bumph', taught in British schools all over the place. Starting his reign as a devout Catholic in the year 1509 AD, Henry challenged the Papacy's assumed power in England by the year 1532 AD, when it refused to condone the annulment of his marriage to Catherine of Aragon. On subsequently marrying Anne Boleyn bygamously anyway, he banished the Papacy from the whole of England, commandeering all of its properties to his realm. Hypocritically he remained a true Catholic, in the sense of his continuance of Catholic dictums, ceremonies and protocols, duly perpetuating all of its conventional rituals, of 'confessions', of 'confirmations' etc. All of which was disconcerting – to the say the least – for Thomas More, Henry 8th's Lord Chancellor. More was a Catholic zealot, strongly affiliated to the Catholic 'Third Order Of St Francis' in England. Long standing, he opposed any sort of Popish rebellion, most particularly the ongoing 'Protestant Reformation'. In the meantime in Europe 'to-be', Desiderius Erasmus created a Greek language version of 'The New Testament'. An event that marked the beginning of the end of the Papacy's stranglehold on Christian ecclesiastic literature. The Bible - with all of its related thesis – up to that time in England, was available solely in Roman Latin. Subsequently, the Papacy's agents – priest, bishops and archbishops – had monopolised its interpretation, due to the scarcity of persons able to read Latin.

Prior to these events, Thomas More had drawn swords – intellectually speaking – with William Tyndale. A 'giant' of English literature evolvements, ominously unrecognised in modern history media. As a new priest, Tyndale soon conflicted with his colleagues – more so his superiors – in relation to the prevailing Catholic attitudes of his time. All of the Pope's subjects –

all of the minions - were directed to pay their penances to God as church congregants. They were directed to worship in the midst of the Catholic dictums of the age, all of which were orchestrated by the Pope's agents as they masqueraded as Godly saviours. During these times, resistance and rebellion invoked deplorable punishments to incite terror in the minds of the 'unholy'. Then, death penalties were imposed on all that defied this religious order, much in the same vein as – king betrayal - 'treason' retributions. When Henry 8th ascended to the English throne – in accordance with the traditions of the 'Holy Roman Empire' – the monarch and the Papacy were synonymous. By the precedent of king John 1st - opposing Magna Carta - an affront on the king was an affront on the Papacy, and an affront on the Papacy was an affront on the monarch. Such integration was reflected during Henry 8th's early rule with the prominence of Cardinal Wolsley, who was also the 'Lord Chancellor'. The Monarch and the Papacy were one of the same. Far ahead of his time, Tyndale saw the folly of the subjugation approach. As a staunch 'Godly' person, he was much frustrated with all of the 'holy' obedience dictums, with few people in England able to read the Bible. Opposing the order of things during his time, he was forced to vacate to Germany, to Martin Luther's land. There he conceived – in its original context, as a true pioneer – the concept of 'winning hearts and minds'. His aim then, was to promote widespread 'belief' in – as opposed to obedience to – God, to be achieved by creating a new English Bible, which could be understood by all of the underling minions in England.

By the year 1530 AD – as a banished refugee under the threat of death – Tyndale was busying himself expeditiously with the translation of Desiderius Erasmus's pure Greek version of the new testament, into Chaucer styled English, much pioneering many English phrases and junctures, eventually to form the basis of current English in its modern form. Truly – until his death in the year 1536 AD – Tyndale pursued a pedantic mission, spurted with immense determination and resourcefulness. He even managed the wholesale printing of his 'archetype' English Bible, which he and his supporters successfully smuggled into England and Scotland. This was read zealously and it was 'grapewined' all about England in the face of widespread Papacy resistance. In the meantime however, due to Henry 8th's animosities with the Papacy in Rome, Thomas More – with his unshaken Popish allegiances – found himself in the chair of persecution, just as Tyndale had found himself after authoring 'The Practyse of Prelates' which opposed Henry 8th's divorce from Catherine of Aragon. However, times were truly changing in England. With Tyndale's subsequent authorship of 'The Obedience of a Christian Man' which supported monarchial sovereignty within regencies, over the Papacy, Henry ceased to be a religious hypocrite; more a Tyndale disciple. By which time, he had gained opportunities to read Tyndale's English language version of the 'New Testament'. To which, he may have been converted? Subsequently, he removed all Catholic Latin versions of the Bible from the churches of England, later to be replaced largely, with augmented Tyndale versions.

Where Tyndale in reality, educated Henry 8th – lifting him out of Hell into spiritualism – he never gained legitimacy in his eyes. Most probably, this was due to his damnation of Henry's 'Catherine of Aragon' divorce actions. Thus, Henry was virulent

41

in the suppression of the evidence of his achievements. Worse for Tyndale, he was eventually abducted, imprisoned and murdered by Catholics zealots, never to be acknowledged. Similarly, Thomas More – in the midst of all of Henry 8th's 'blood' rages - was beheaded in the tower of London. Interestingly, by the year 1935 AD, More prevailed in history media, duly canonised by Pope Pius 11th, as a martyr of the schism of the Anglican/Catholic church separation. In the same media, of Tyndale, no mention. Consider this though, the whole of Tyndale's Greek to English new testament and nine sections of his unfinished Hebrew to English old testament were adapted for the creation of Henry 8th's 'Great Bible', commissioned by him in the year 1535 AD, just a year before Tyndale's death. All of which was attributed to Myles Coverdale, a scholar more to Henry's liking. Many of Tyndale's translations were available for copying by that time, due to his successful smuggling operations, but hundreds of them were burned as seditious literature. Ironically and somewhat ominously, the incomplete sections of Tyndale's old testament were translated from Latin to English, and thus, were less authentic. Think of this further: Tyndale – a renowned scholar of his day – translated from Greek and Hebrew to English with remarkable expertise, in a style that suited illiterates with limited abilities of comprehension. His work is full of simple – but profoundly clear – words and phrases, not of his making, but of his comprehension as a Greek language and a Hebrew language scholar. He exhibited rare English language expertise, not inherent in the abilities of subsequent revisers of the English Bible, least of all Myles Coverdale. With all of the populace – all of the underling minions – of England attending the churches – listening to

Tyndale's simply written scriptures – as indeed they all did by the year 1590 AD, the English language – in its written form – exploded to new unprecedented dimensions. Profoundly in time for all of Shakespear's subsequent enhancements. Within all of these circumstances, of old, the 'establishment' of England venerated its true inclinations to grant credence to 'patronage', 'favour' and 'connivance', in the face of 'merit' denial. Here, my contentions about the prevelance of this atmosphere – in the midst of 'the establishment' – are strongly corroborated.

Section Eleven:
Papacy Struggles In The Lands Of Europe 'To-Be'

In addition to all of these occurrences in England – and Scotland with English Bible infiltrations abound – Henry 8th was also heretic of the 'Holy Roman Empire' because profoundly important religious events occurred within the Pope's domain during his reign. Essentially, he was heretic because - unlike all of his predecessors – he could be, due to the Pope in Rome – and Catholicism – losing exclusive godly sanction. Quite certainly during this era, a lot of important people were horrified by the inherent corruptive influence of the Hapsburgs, Spain and all of its corrupting colonial expansions, in pursuit it seemed, of gold before God or the Bible. To which, the Pope in Rome was conspicuously implicated. By the time Henry 8th in England was king, Roman Catholicism – and particularly the Papacy – was being seriously challenged in the Germanies by Martin Luther, and more so within two decades afterwards by Huldrych Zwingli. Likewise in the Franka lands by John Calvin. The outcome was the strong establishment of a new 'protestant' religious order

– albeit a somewhat convoluted one - within the domain of the 'Holy Roman Empire', which really, Henry 8th in England sided with by sacking the Papacy's monasteries, and by founding the Anglican church. All later augmented with the establishment of Presbyterianism in Scotland by John Knox. This order did not displace Christianity. Retrospectively analysed, it removed – quite distinctively – the Papacy – and therefore the Hapsburgs – from English holiness, having been already eradicated in the western regions of Westfalia and Swcheslic Holstein. It also drew swords with the filthy rich – and the incomprehensively corrupt – Medici empire in Italy.

Yet, the 'Reformation' – as it is identified nowadays – even with all of Henry 8th's aspirations and vilifications, did not altogether occur suddenly. Martin Luther's and John Calvin's transformation was not witnessed in its total fruition in their lifetimes, or indeed Henry 8th's lifetime. More significantly the 'Reformation' was really born during the lifetime of Jan Hus. From him evolved the 'Hussites'. Of no particular class or creed within Moravia, these people were the first to break with the Papacy in Rome. The 'Holy Roman Empire' – with a mixed international army - even launched a crusade against them in the year 1431 AD, which failed. With subsequent persecutions over many years, their 'pure' credences were renewed – with the assistance of invading Swedes - by the year 1722 AD in Herrnhut, Saxony, and by the year 1740 AD they were active as Red Indian Missionaries in North America. The birth of the Hussites, Martin Luther's 'Ninety-Five Thesis' and the birth of John Calvin's 'Calvinist' faith – all Christian with pure and simple causes – evolved because of the conspiracy between the Papacy, the Medici dynasty and the

Hapsburg dynasty, in particular between Pope Leo X(the second son of Giovanni de Medici), Giovanni de Medici(leader at the time of the Medici dynasty) and Charles 1st of Spain(also at the time, Charles V of the Holy Roman Empire). Charles 1st of Spain, the first culpable invader of the South American continent, sacking its ancient civilisations and – through Portuguese extensions – converting Brazil – big time – into a land of slaves. Giovanni de Medici, a pioneer – as a banking magnate – of wealth accumulation without proportionate work effort, spreading decadence, power and glory, within range of all of Florence's and Rome's infrastructures. Some of the world's most revered art emanated from Medici extravagance, such as frescoes produced by Michelangelo in the Sistine Chapel, Rome. Pope Leo 10th, the debaucher that extravagantly commissioned nudist art to adorn Vatican architecture, and who promoted 'indulgence' sales(payment for sins to the 'Vatican See').

The battle in England and Scotland with Catholicism, continued throughout the reign of Henry's successor, Elizabeth 1st. With Mary(Queen of Scots) – a devout catholic – vying for monarchical power, Elizabeth and her subjects witnessed profound changes within Christian lands – or more particularly in seas dominated by Christians – due to the evolvement of 'navies', of the Spanish and of the English kind. With Francis Drake's remarkable trans-world voyage in the Golden Hind - completed by the year 1580 AD - and with Drake's skirmishing exploits against Spanish galleons, war – and the domination of minions – became more about big wooden sailing ships, laden with powerful – but heavy – canons. The gunpowder age had arrived, with destruction truly ratcheted upwards. The subsequent defeat of

Philip 2nd's naval armada – carrying troops to invade England – placed the English navy – with all of its successive 1st Sea Lords - into the pinnacles of political power, supremely and perpetually to this day.

Yet in the end, it was not the monarchs of Britain or even the stalwarts of the new found 'Protestants' that brought about the 'beginning of the end' of the Holy Roman Empire. Napoleon Bonaparte is credited mostly here, in this regard. In the meantime, the Spanish empire of the Hapsburgs and the Papacy, declined decisively, particularly because 'gold' in abundance – imported into Spain from south America – corrupted all that were complicit. It also influenced inclinations in Spain to import durable goods – in preference to manufacturing them – over an extended period, much reducing Spain's economic institutions and its manufacturing infrastructure. Yet the Hapsburgs and the Papacy retained enough strength in the face of protestant 'Lutherism' and 'Calvinism' in the Christian world, to bolster the ambitions of Charles 1st of England, to please his wife with strives to establish supreme regency power in the face of a devoutly strong English 'Protestant' Parliament. Not wholly realised by Charles though, his subjects – through the efforts of Henry 8th and Elizabeth 1st – inherited, along with him, a 'Parliament', formed of commoners and lords to jointly power share. To jointly extol all of the interests of the king and the Anglican church(in the House of Lords) and to protect the welfare of the common people(in the House of Commons). With the House of Commons formed more or less exclusively from the wealthy land owning fraternity, reality was far from the latter ideal however. Yet, all was better than being slaves overseered by the Hapsburgs and with all of England overseered by the Papacy. Not realising this initially, Charles discovered that all of it was so, eventually.

In contemporary Britain, a battle of the sexes is quite definitely raging, with a prevailing fear of eventual devastation in the minds of sophisticated thinkers. When I was a boy, the concept of 'children should be seen but not heard' was strong and widespread. Never being invited to express any sort of opinion - like most other minors - I often found myself within hearing range of rivalries between the genders of adults, at home most of the time, but occasionally elsewhere too. At that time, the environment was simpler by far. People fitted into distinct categories in accordance with their gender and their class. There were those that possessed material wealth and there were those that didn't. Those that had gained more opportunities to consolidate themselves through better education and with easier access to professional careers, and those that were forced to accept miserly payment for arduous physical effort. I remember distinctly, that most 'workers' in factories, mines, at marine docks and in mills, pursued 'overtime' - just to acquire extras – with zeal. Truly trapped in massive institutions of toil for seven days a week, enhanced subsistence was the limit of aspiration for the majority of the Queen's subjects during the 1950s and the 1960s. In fact, this phenomenon strongly influenced my contention to find a better existence than cycling three or four miles or so through the rush hour traffic in Preston, twice a day, with a pack of sandwiches and a thermos flask in my satchel. Just to toil – repetitively and relentlessly – in some sort of 'production institution'. In the end, I joined the Royal Air Force, finding myself in the Far East before I was 19 years old. Having been discouraged from putting in a serious effort to pass the 'eleven plus' examination – because it was against my father's political principles – and after being forced to attend one of the most deplorable secondary schools in the country, this to me, was the most sensible expedient to follow.

Section Twelve:
Notorious Social Class and Gender Divisions:

Deeply embedded in the 'have nots' social class of this country as a boy, I was always told – or rather, most of the time it was inferred – that I was lowly and that I should know my place. Being lowly, I must be of low mental abilities. All of this was in the air in those days and it was applied equally to both genders of the deprived classes. Contrastingly, the posh types were always glorified, most of the time being accredited with abilities that they did not really possess. You see, I saw all of this when I joined the Royal Air Force. Then I encountered 'men' and 'boys' from every niche of Great Britain and from every ancestral origin. When at first I attempted to enter, the selectors told me that I was not educated enough and that I should go away and return at a later date. When I refused, they just placed me in a lowly trade. Yet then, more opportunities were available to me than my contemporaries, of opposite gender. Then, girls at the age of sixteen years could not enter the Royal Air Force at all. Then though – in contrast to the current period – they did not really want to. The girls – the young women – of the deprived classes, just wondered about getting themselves pregnant, and then grieved year in, year out, due to their babies being – universally – adopted. Inevitably, most subsequently adapted by 'existing' in factories and mills until they could start afresh by marrying someone with secure employment.

It is my perception that gender rivalry has always existed in this nation, but women – much more than men – have historically been slaves of their souls. Devoted to their sons, and most often, to some sort of religious faith. Victims of their maternal instincts, they are forced to seek repentance for their sins. They have to cleanse themselves, they have to suffer to gain salvation. Most of all, they have to make sacrifices to make amends for their delinquency years, within which they knew no bounds of morality. There is nothing like the wrath of a vicar's daughter, who through transgression becomes a 'do good' stalwart. This sort of history just repeats itself, time and again. Most remarkably – and profoundly – what women cannot achieve themselves, they will achieve through their sons, or if they are totally sexist, they will achieve through any of their children, particularly through their daughters. Where my father was a stalwart of the 'anti-Christ', his second wife – my step mother who conspired with an adulterer(my father) - characteristically subordinated me in order to 'ascend' her own real sons; inevitably! Yet 'fate' prevails, always. Even my father must have wondered about spiritual forces being out their somewhere, mapping all of our lives like pawns in a grand chess game. Soon after leaving my father and his iniquitous spouse, I learned to drive by smashing a car that I stole into parked vehicles along an urban suburb in Birmingham, and by gallivanting with cheap old cars around the rural roads of Norfolk. At a later time however, the elder of my half siblings conceived by my step-mother was killed in a head-on vehicle collision. Did she ever wonder whether this outcome was 'retribution'? Having deliberately been dispassionate, forfeiting the gift of a son, one of her own blood perished for ever. At that time – and for time immemorial – she was unable to regain what she had forfeited.

In the midst of all of the conflicts of sexism – within which sons and daughters extrapolate – within marriages particularly, 'who wears the trousers?' has become a defunct question. With the substantial decline of the institution of marriage, it is asked less and less. Anyway, women wear trousers most of the time nowadays. The literal sense of it has disappeared. The shift towards the equality of genders during the last five decades has been so considerable in this country, that contemporary feminists – and there are still lots of them – are seen – in the eyes of many men – as strivers for gender dominance. 'Who wears the trousers?' however, relates - as of old – to strength of character, selfishness, arrogance, vanity and personal intelligence. Unlike their predecessors, contemporary British women of the dominating kind are less able – due to the diminishment of male power - to operate in a clandestine way, forcefully under their husband's cloaks.

Section Thirteen:
The First National Civil War In Europe:

Having first attempted to marry into the Spanish Hapsburg dynasty unsuccessfully – which of course meant that he would also have had to become a catholic convert – Charles 1st eventually married into his contemporary French catholic dynasty, ceasing to quell the strong catholic convictions of his spouse, who was in due course, also complicit in attacks on the English parliament. Where Charles was the official head of state in England, it appeared that true national leadership actually emanated from his wife, who was very influential in dissolving and ignoring – for eleven years – successive parliaments. Certainly, Charles was not at all interested in sharing the control of his subjects. Through a long period he connived to avoid compromise, even resurrecting unfair taxes on shipping to work independently apart from Parliament. Really though, it was his unwillingness to quell a strong catholic revival within his realm that sewed the seeds of rebellion against him. Then, the influences of Martin Luther and John Calvin were solidly entrenched, and they were widely practiced within the bounds of the Anglican church and Protestantism. Charles attempted to persecute Sir Thomas Fairfax, Henry Ireton and Oliver Cromwell – all prominent Parliamentarians – but soon discovered that they were able to rally significant opposition, which eventually – because of Cromwell's innovative interventions – evolved as the 'Parliamentary Army, otherwise known as 'The Roundheads'.

At first, preliminary skirmishes occurred between the 'Roundheads' and the king's 'Cavaliers', but really matters had to be settled on the basis of supporting numbers – as to Parliament and as to the King – in head-on combat. Although cavalry and footmen – of equal numbers - comprised the initial fighting forces, soldier discipline and weapons innovation – imposed and devised by Cromwell – provided early Parliamentarian advantages in the mammoth battles of Marston Moor(1644) and Naseby(1645). Famously, Cromwell's 'Pike Men' stood firm in the face of Prince Rupert's charging cavalry. Long strong pikes held by disciplined men – in large congregated numbers – were immovable by swashbuckling horse mounted swordsmen, of the kind fighting for Charles and Rupert. With the successful quelling of the royal army – and with the king eventually executed for recruiting foreign enemies to fight against his own compatriots - Cromwell then campaigned with his Roundheads, all around the lands of England, Scotland and Ireland, ruthlessly displacing all of the king's favoured royalists, shored up for battle in their castles, their mansions and their manors. Not particularly as formidable as they had been of old, due to gunpowder and canons, fired most often during the civil war by very experienced Dutch mercenaries, used often by Cromwell. Thus, nearly every castle in these lands stand now as ruins. What came out of it all? The new nation of Britain, embracing Scotland and Ireland, where real unions had not existed beforehand. Also, the new 'Commonwealth' with the colonialisation of the West Indies, Trinidad and Tobago, and numerous other foreign lands. In the midst of wars with the newly founded nation of 'The Nederland(1648)', the new 'Commonwealth' was important, because its existence hindered the 'Dutch East Indies Company', which by the turn of the 17th/18th centuries, placed 'The Nederland' as a world economic power.

The son of Charles 1st of England, Charles 2nd, on the death knell of the magnanimous Oliver Cromwell, re-established a somewhat modified royal form of rule in England eventually. Ironically – in a dastardly fashion some would say – one of the prime sewers of the original republican seeds, Sir Thomas Fairfax, invited him back to England. In this way, the existing French 'Bourbon' dynasty – which significantly, later brought Louis 16th into the world – was strengthened. Importantly however, religious worshippers loyal to the Pope in Rome were not persecuted during Cromwell's time. Cromwell reigned and he conquered, and then he delegated his hard won political power back to Parliament, more than once. As a reluctant overseer, he was the principal exponent, not only of democracy but also of unity between the English, the Scots, the Welsh and the Irish, forming the 'Commonwealth', which later evolved as the 'United Kingdom of Great Britain' by the year 1707 AD. All was made possible, only because he decimated – with canons - all of the royalist sub-regencies in the land, in order to establish Parliament as a single national executor. With subsequent formations, even Charles 2nd was unable to turn the clock back to regain the prominence that his recent ancestors had enjoyed. Where the castles were the emblems of power, they could not exist in the face of canons. After they were destroyed, the rulers of the regions that collectively constituted the king's regency became impotent. In this context, the destruction of 'power infrastructures' remains to this day, one of the prime goals of war mongers.

Many precedents were established during Cromwell's time and a number of important conclusions are to be drawn about the outcomes of all wars, first becoming apparent during the English civil war. The first – and foremost – is that the Papacy's infrastructure – what was left after Henry 8th sacked the monasteries – escaped untouched and fairly well intact. Whereas all of the substantial infrastructure – principally the castles – built and refined by the slaves of successive monarchs from the year 1066 AD onwards, were reduced to ruins. This was truly the result of a political war with the British regency, waged by Cromwell. Executed with amazing consistency throughout the land by means of gun powder and canons. In Bristol – Prince Rupert's domicile of folly – the formidable castle was reduced to virtually 'nothing', due to canon balls raining onto it from the top of Brandon hill. In the process, a lot of innocent civilians were harmed, just because they were at the scene, unable to escape. The Parliamentary thrust however was – consistently - directed at the protective infrastructure of the king's exponents, and inevitably at all supporters of these exponents. All within the national boundary however. In principle, the Parliamentarians fought the monarch, not the Holy Roman Empire. In reality however, the monarch – Charles 1st – was extraordinarily influenced by his spouse, who through her family connections, was strongly allied to the Pope in Rome, who in turn remained in cahoots with the 'Holy Roman Empire'.

Section Fourteen:
War Ethics And Legacies:

Still listening to adult conversations when I was a boy, the issue of war and destruction arose on many occasions, in my home and in the midst of political affrays conducted by my father with his friends. Just how remarkable it was that 'the architectural infrastructure of the Papacy had survived the English civil war', was never a particular topic, because he remained ignorant of it all. For all of the time that I lived under his umbrella, I never saw him pick up a book. He wrote a lot – in his usual extrovertial way – but he did not read. Of working class origins, he was uneducated. Yet – through word of mouth and conjecture – he knew a lot about the modern 'repetitions' of the 'English Civil War-Papacy Survival' phenomenon. Although he didn't actually graduate into 'combat' during the WW2 period, word had been passed to him about the manic bombing of Monte-Casino, and about the annihilation of numerous German cities, particularly Koln(Cologne). In contrast to the Cromwell era, in his young days, a grapevine sourced social network was well established in Britain. It had told him all about the remarkable survival of St Paul's cathedral in London during the 'Blitz', although I am sure to this day that he remained totally unaware of the significance of this outcome. The reasons for it to me are obvious. As a place of Christian worship of old – with a distinctive Thomas Becket legacy – German bombing crews deliberately missed it, even in the face of Hitler's compulsions to obliterate the British people. Many of the members of these crews were Christians, still closely allied to the Papacy.

It has also been argued – with some foundation – that the cathedrals of Koln(Cologne) and Notre Dame(de Paris) similarly survived Churchill's/Hariss's 1,000 bomber raids, of which many occurred during 1944/45. They were deliberately missed. Moreso, the Vatican in Rome was officially protected, never being defined as an official target, and also widely avoided by allied aircraft pilots, with the exception of an incident with a renegade American pilot that released bombs onto the garden of the 'Holy See'. WW2 in Europe was definitely a political war, not a religious one. The total destruction of Monte Casino by allied bombing does not contradict this conclusion. Such action was justifiable – in the name of Christ and in the name of civilisation – because German paratroopers made specific use of it, in attempts to protect themselves.

With all of the monasteries obliterated, and then with all of royal infrastructures – the castles – in a shambles, even with Catholicism being widely tolerated – in accordance with Oliver Cromwell's legacy – Charles II, on gaining royal status, did not display inclinations to challenge the sovereignty of the Anglican church in England, or the Presbyterian church in Scotland and Wales during his short rule. A factor difficult to absorb because his mother was a Papacy zealot, to the end. Also, because he intruded into England with an army during Cromwell's reign, to establish an insurrection in the year 1651 AD, which failed at Worcester. Nine years later however - with the prospects of his long-desired aims being realised peacefully – he issued his 'Breda' documents to Parliament in England, conceding numerous land rights, and rights of religious conscience. In so doing, he acknowledged the sovereignty of Parliament as the principal arbitrator of all of the minions in England, and – somewhat ominously – he accepted that the royal throne of England could only be held by a protestant monarch in accordance with the legacies of Henry 8th and Elizabeth 1st. At this time, England, Scotland and Wales were unique, not just in the context of the rest of the European land mass – which was still in the main, indirectly subjected to regency infiltrated Papacy influence – but also in the context of the whole of the world. In these lands for the first time ever, all of the minions – the surfs, the paupers and all of the aristocracy of the old order – were controlled by an elected Parliament. Methods of patronage – of old – prevailed however, with nepotism and wealth-geared privilege remaining entrenched. All of the land – generating all of the available wealth by means of farming – remained in the hands of the ancestors of the Norman barons of old, providing them with obscene levels of wealth, and influence within the national system of administration. The 'establishment' remained corrupt, decadent and unduly belligerent, and the minions remained impoverished, deprived and destitute.

After all of this – within just three years of the death of Charles 2nd – the wrath of Henrietta Maria – the spouse of Charles 1st and the mother of Charles 2nd – splurged and rippled through England like a tsunami. As a spited zealot of Catholicism – and as a devoted agent of the 'Holy Roman Empire' – she witnessed the placement of her second son on the English throne, James 2nd. Truly within range of his mother's war chants, he conspired to place Catholics in high offices in the military and elsewhere, and he also attempted to suspend the powers of his mother's arch enemy: Parliament. Yet Parliament as a concept in England and Wales was too entrenched to be susceptible to insurrection. It passed the 'Test' act, enforcing the exclusive placement of 'Church of England' worshippers to high office. Additionally, with the birth of James's son, anti-catholic mania evolved within the general populace. With the unusual persistence of the legacy of Elizabeth 1st, Mary 2nd of the Nederland – the protestant sister of James 2nd – received requests to take up the English throne with her Dutch husband William 3rd. When they arrived with a substantial army, James fled to France. Yet within a decade - by the year 1690 AD – matters to do with the tolerance of Papacy influences – Catholicism – were still not settled. Rallying supporting armies in France and Ireland, James attacked the ardent protestants of Northern Ireland as an initial means of regaining the lands that he forfeited to William 3rd, in England. All culminated into the notorious 'Battle of the Boyne', at the Boyne river, just south of Armagh, Northern Ireland. With William's soldiers victorious in this battle, James returned to France, forever exiled, just like his mother. From that time – until the Good Friday agreement was reached in the year 1997 AD until 'now', religiously biased conflicts – often requiring military intervention – have persisted repetitively and relentlessly in this region. Even the stalwart UK premier Margaret Thatcher was threatened - near to death - in the 'Brighton Bombing', as a consequence of these conflicts. With the eventual death of William 3rd in the year 1702 AD, his spouse Anne – daughter of James 2nd – ascended to the throne of England, consolidating the original regency union between England and Scotland. This theme of consolidation continued during her reign with Parliamentary union between these dominions being established with the 'Act of Union' in the year 1707 AD.

Section Fifteen:
Reformation Struggles:

Taking Parliament – born in the early 14th century - as a growing force that has steadfastly extenuated the protestant legacy of Elizabeth 1st, political England is traditionally distinct from the rest of Europe. However, it has been closely allied with Calvin and Luthernian protestant elements in The Nederland. These alliances originate from the strive for Dutch independence from the Spanish 'Hapsburg' dynasty during Elizabeth's reign. This was realistically achieved by the year 1579 AD in the form of 'The United Provinces of the Nederland, in the midst of extended conflicts between the Spanish-Hapsburg dynasty and the Dutch within Dutch provincial boundaries. Embedded in the Spanish army in The Nederland at the close of this period, Guy Fawkes – an English catholic convert and zealot opposing protestants, returned to England. Utilising the superior technology of his day – gunpowder – he attempted to destroy the English Parliamentary building, with all of the Parliamentarians in it. Characteristic of that time – with retribution/punishment being used as the potent element of the control of all of the minions – he was burned to death by means of a bonfire during January of the year 1606 AD. Such was the order of the period, and such was the struggle against the 'Holy Roman Empire'. Ironically – especially within the view of Francis Drake's great exploits – the Dutch, on gaining independence, utilised Spanish maritime technology and maritime navigation know-how – which really was subsequent of Portuguese maritime know-how – to discover and to exploit the East Indies, eventually forming the Dutch East Indies Company, greatly to their economic benefit. The company successfully kept the source of its shipped imports secret, generating considerable international rivalry. By the time Mary 2nd of the Nederland arrived in England as a new monarch, Holland was still ascending in the world as a major economic power. Then also, it held a virtual monopoly in grain-to-baking flower production, due to the utilisation of superior wind-mill technology. Additionally – in line with their maritime developments – the Dutch were leading canon shooters, used in the guise of mercenaries by Oliver Cromwell, to demolish the castles of the rebellious royals during England's civil war.

Of all of the profound events in history, world-wide, in Britain, the burning of the 'Guy Fawkes' effigy is foremost in the minds of all of the minions, although the meaning of the traditional firework extravaganza has changed. When I was boy, begging was legal – and even popular – in the context of placing an old rag-doll effigy of 'Guy' in a defunct perambulator, wheeled around in the depths of shopping streets and omnibus stations. "A penny for the Guy" the boys used to shout – and many pennies they used to get – because – due to the impressions of things that I formed in those days – the 'Guy' effigy and the poor boy combination invoked a strange sort of sympathy for the deprived and the persecuted. Then in the late 1950s, all working people knew that state persecution for none conformance – and especially, rebellion – was the way of things, from old. Bonfire night – but moreso, poor boys begging – re-kindled these conceptions, year by year. Even then, most of the minions – giving pennies to begging Guy Fawkes boys – didn't fully understand the reasons for the November 5th celebrations. They just knew that Parliament had been threatened, and that such a threat was regarded by those in the higher echelons, to be significant. Progressive logic therefore identified Parliament as a building – and as an institution – that was precious, forever to be preserved. Very few – if at all any – in that 5th decade of the 20th century knew that the Guy Fawkes incident was born of religious conflict. Almost all thought then, that it had been about politics. However, easily by the 1950s the British state was a secular one, as indeed it remains to this day. During the final stages of the 17th century however, political/religious divisions were not so distinct. Boys begging on the streets with Guy Fawkes effigies have since, dissolved away, because children nowadays within the majority of our societies are provided for, much more generously by their parents. With them, all of the semblances of the Guy Fawkes event have dissolved also. All that is left of 'fireworks night' is fireworks, of the modern kind that create fantasia in the sky, extravagantly; all fantastic. Gone are the reminders of poor people, begging for pennies. Gone is the reminder that – of old, by the barons and the lords of old – punishment for rebellion was often cruel and dastardly, as of the burning of human flesh on a bonfire.

While it springs to mind, my memories of the 1950s decade also include my astonishment at some day-to-day scenes that I have since identified as common remnants of the 'Holy Roman Empire'. Particularly, I remember a number of my school friends being over-awed with the importance – in the whole context of their lives – with their opportunities to participate in 'Holy Communion', on their acceptance through 'Confirmation' into their local Roman Catholic church. With a sensible comparative view of these people then, they were seriously deprived – like myself – boded in the midst of 'mill worker' dwellings, back-to-back, separated only with walled yards and back alleys, with cats howling and scurrying at night. They bathed in iron tubs in front of the only fire that they could afford to burn. They used old newspapers for toilet paper – in their outdoor water closets, of course – and their animal pets suffered often with all sorts of strange afflictions – such as St Vitaces's Dance, a compulsive twitching disorder – because the PDSA(Peoples Dispensary for Sick Animals) was not about prominently then. Then, it was commonly George Orwell's 'Road to Wigan Pier' in Preston, Lancashire, England, with poor Catholics abound. A niche of the old order of things. Truly a niche of the old 'Holy Roman Empire'. Often, after visiting these friends I used to strive up New Hall Lane towards home, passing their church. Stood there, with all of its laboriously stained glass windows, with its magnificent pillars, with all of its gold and silver ornamentia and with all of its finely crafted wood-work, it was megalomania to me. The ostentatious priest was often to be seen arriving in his big expensive limousine, robed for glory and braced for Mary Magdalene, waltzing – almost flying - in the wind into his immodest mansion, adjacent to his glory den of God. He muttered: "I'm alright Jack", perhaps?

Make no mistake about it, some of the populace of the 'European' continental land mass – as the 17th century dawned, and as Guy Fawkes sizzled – had already irreversibly altered environments elsewhere in the world, through a number of preceding decades. Economic forces were gathering pace, spurred by the enterprising Dutch that utilised rare and exotic spices from the east of the world in a far more lucrative manner than the Spanish with their gold from the South Americas. To come – beyond Elizabeth 1st's and Philip 2nd' of Spain's life span – was a holocaust throughout Europe, born of the repressive stranglehold of the 'Holy Roman Empire' and born of conflicting regencies stretching from the Atlantic coasts of France in the west, to Ottoman territory – beyond Hungary 'to-be' – in the east, and from Sweden in the north to Sicily in the south. At the centre of it all – and geographically at the centre of the European land mass in the region of what is now the German nation - the southern principalities of Bavaria and Baden Wuttenburg rallied with the Spanish and the Austrian Hapsburg dynasties, to stem Lutheran religious rebellions against the Papacy, which had occurred spasmodically but regularly, with the growing strength of Lutheran and Calvin doctrines. Mixed up in all of the religious paraphernalia of the time, economic forces – particularly those appertaining to international trade – generated earnest rivalry between the Hapsburg dynasty – prevailing in

Spain, Austria, and with the support of the Papacy in Rome – and united principality groups in Sweden 'to-be' and 'The Nederland'. Where the Swedish elements were religiously motivated in sympathy with a Christian 'Protestant' religious reformation, the Dutch were of course driven more to rebel against – and to extricate – the Hapsburgs to protect their economic interests.

For thirty years between the years 1618-1648 successive wars raged mainly in the heartlands of what would eventually become Germany, with the Swedes marauding all around, and with Von Count Johann Tilly leading the Hapsburg's 'Catholic League' against them. Tilly successfully besieged and sacked the Protestant city of Magdeburg, at the time that Charles 1st reigned exclusively in England with a prevailing contempt for his Parliament. Yet within fourteen years, the Hapsburg's 'Holy Roman Empire' – in the heart of Germany to-be - transformed into numerous independent 'Protestant' principalities, confirmed with legally signed treaties. The Swedes gained control over the Baltic, The Nederland was affirmed as a completely independent nation, likewise, the Swiss Confederation became Switzerland, and the border between France and the Germanies was clearly defined at the Rhine river. All was concluded during peace negotiations at Westfalia in the year 1648 AD, much to the distaste of Ferdinand 2nd, king of Hungary, emperor of the 'Holy Roman Empire' and the archduke of Austria. Yet at this juncture, the entity of Germany – as it was known immediately prior to WW1 – was still a fractured mosaic styled land mass, far from evolving as a single nation. In the meantime – just one year after the conclusion of the thirty year wars in Europe – Charles 1st in England had been executed and the English civil war was virtually concluded. In this context, the influence of Catholicism throughout the whole of Europe diminished considerably, but significantly, literacy – the realm of real knowledge transfer – was still monopolised by the Christian ecclesiastic world. Not for long however. Most particularly, Cromwell's Britain soon to become 'The British Commonwealth' was then a 'political' domain, unlike the rest of Europe, which resolutely embroiled itself with religious issues, religious conflicts and religiously biased authority over most of the minions within it.

Section Sixteen:
The First Nations Of Europe:

This situation was characteristically the same in France – with a considerable portion of its populace Protestant reformed – facing Hapsburg belligerence from time to time during the Thirty Years War. However – in contrast to most of the European land mass of the period – France under Louis 13th existed with its monarchy – crudely – reigning with the accompaniment of a Parliament(Parlement) comprising principality, princes from all over the land. Also, the ruling 'royal' regime was infiltrated strongly by the Hapsburg Dynasty when Louis 13th married Anne of Austria(of the house of Hapsburg). Anne was the daughter of Philip 3rd of Spain and Margaret of Austria, important emissaries of the Hapsburg legacy. When Louis 13th died in 1643 his heir – Louis 14th – was too young to rule, requiring his mother Anne to rule as his regent until he came of age. Really, the plot had been concocted – within the bounds of the 'Holy Roman Empire', with its strong Papacy connections – by the Hapsburgs, to vigorously influence French rule. Jules Mazarin – originally one of the Pope's diplomats attending the French royal court – found himself in favour with Louis 13th and the Papacy, on successfully quelling rule succession conflicts between France and Spain. Of Italian descent, he became a naturalised French subject and soon afterwards, was granted significant stature as a 'Cardinal' by the Papacy. On the death of Louis 13th in the year 1643 AD – to the delight of the Hapsburgs – Anne, the new regent monarch, appointed him as France's first minister. With all of the power that this appointment brought – and with Anne rarely involving herself with French politics - the 'Frondes' of 'Parlement' and of the 'Princes' evolved. These were 'coup-d'etat' insurrection attempts against the monarchy, led during the 'Fronde of the Princes' by Prince Louis Conde of Bourbon. With all of the princes of France unified under his leadership in opposition to Mazarin, Anne's – and her son Louis 14th's – positions were precariously threatened. In the event, Anne, Mazarin and Louis were forced to leave Paris, but they returned victoriously after their supporters defeated Conde's army in the years 1652-3 AD.

On his return to Paris, Marzarin exercised absolute political power in France until his death in the year 1661 AD, even after Louis graduated – as he became of age – as the legal monarch. Marzarin the dictator, that attempted to re-convert all of the French protestants back to Catholicism. What came of it? Louis 14th the 'absolute' monarch, of course. Louis 14th with delusions of grandeur, builder of the palace of 'Versailles' and the invader of the north American continent. The palace of 'Versailles', what an irony and what a travesty this later became. Louis 14th, a re-aggressor against the Nederland and a grand-styled persecutor of all of the protestants within his lands, corrupted with the privileges of royal status, over more than six decades(1638-1715 AD). By the time of his death, France was – even if reluctantly - a fully unified nation, just as far as the control of all of its principalities were concerned. Louis forced all of his princes to depend on him, within his grandeur realm, within the 'Palace of Versailles', even throughout the new lands that his military forces had invaded in the North American continent and about the 'West Indies'. Significantly, like Britain the nation, during the rule of Louis 14th, France asserted itself as a nation powerful enough to vie for lands beyond its borders, building strong armies and a powerful navy. Duly, the boundaries of power in Britain and in France – just like Spain beforehand – extended beyond their motherlands. In the meantime the princes of all of the regencies of Germany 'to-be' and Italy 'to-be' continued to delude themselves about their own particular importance, without really grasping visions of the grand scheme of things. All because they were purely 'Regent' in nature, without any conception of compromise, without accompanying 'Parliaments' and without a force within them all that was able to establish dominance.

Really, at the conclusion of the 17th century, the Germanies were very vulnerable to invasion from the west by France, and from the east by the Hapsburg dynasty in Austria. Both of them were formidable in terms of their resources and in terms of their military organisation. How fortunate they were that Louis 14th focused north and west, on Britain and the north American continent. Even moreso maybe, how fortunate they were that the Austrian Hapsburgs were continuously opposing insertions by the old 'Suleiman' empire of 'Ottoman', raging through 'Bohemia', conquering Hungary and threatening the heart of the Hapsburgs; Vienna, Austria. With a strong sense of the smell of weakness throughout the Germanies, the 18th century progressed into a renewed holocaust for the Austrian Hapsburgs. Actually the Germanies did possess a lion, waiting to pounce. By the year 1740 AD the Prussian king – Frederick 2nd – forcefully extended Prussia into the wealthy Hapsburg territory of Silesia, precluding the infamous 'Seven Years War'. More than ever before, all the minions of future Europe were fodder for imperialistic expansion. Principalities and dominions fused or disappeared through dynasty integrations and through military exploits. New born nations – the United Kingdom and France particularly – ventured into primitive lands beyond their boundaries to vie for dominance. Yet through it all, the structure of all of the societies remained unchanged. Regardless of what principality, what dominion, what nation, all of the underlings were still under-dogs, suppressed and exploited to fight the wars of their masters, to serve as servants, as surfs, as canon fodder, regency adorers, and as Godly worshippers within the realms of 'The Holy Roman Empire'.

Worse, by this time, for centuries the emissaries of Portuguese and the Spanish dynasties had been trading for and enslaving bewildered sub-minions of the coastal regions of Africa, for sugar cane and coffee crop cultivations in Brazil and the West Indies. Additionally, they did likewise to feed labour for cotton cultivations in the southern regions of the north American continent. With the quelling of French military belligerence – culminating in the defeat of Quebec, Canada in the year 1763 AD – and with the widespread establishment of British colonies throughout the north American continent, emissaries of George 3rd – working from the port of Bristol – evolved the infamous 'slave triangle'. Sub-minion Africans were shipped to the southern regions of north America as slave labour for tobacco cultivation. Then the resulting produce was shipped back to Bristol for its minions to process industrially, and for all of Britain's minions to smoke. The result of it all by the 1770s decade remained unaltered for all European minions, absolutely. Significantly, all of the real doers – those that toiled, those that fought and those that contributed to the idolatry of the Papacy – remained illiterate. Likewise, most of those that had jumped the boat over to the new Protestant domain, and who ended up in the midst of numerous skirmishes and wars, that raged on and on for thirty years. Yet with literal skills, new technologies introduced during the early 1700s in Italy, Germany and The Nederland lifted many out of the abyss of ignorance. Regular papers containing critical information were printed by 'movable press techniques' then. New information – 'News' – became tangible and 'confirmable', when these papers were utilised in conjunction with word-of-mouth 'grapevines'. Just a small number of 'literates' converted written 'news' into verbal explanations, to be 'grapevined' all about. This scenario became evident in Britain's north American colonies where literate colony administrators passed urgently sought-after news from the motherland(Britain). With plausible audiences available, James Franklin launched the pioneering 'New-England Courant' newspaper in the year 1721 AD. In motherland Britain however – and throughout the rest of Europe – the uplifting power of printed media remained impotent, due to widespread illiteracy, especially in the midst of the domain of the 'minions', in the midst of the majority of the populace of Europe.

Section Seventeen:
The Birth Of Literary Grapevines:

I understand now – being retired with much more time than I ever had before – that all of the generations in Britain – and everywhere else for that matter – were beset and beleaguered with the scarcity of the ultimate – the most valuable – finite resource of 'time'. Real deep rooted learning takes a lot of time. In the world before the arrival of the 'Internet' it required extensive book reading. A luxury that poor people were always deprived of, from the age when they became aware of the rudiments of literature, to the 1960s decade. This was so because the circumstance of 'poverty' – the power of hunger, and the power of deprivation – forced engagement in the quest of subsistence, which ordinarily consumed most of the time that was available, day-to-day, month-to-month and year-to-year. By the time it was all over, for those that managed to reach a restful 'dusk' in their lives, bodies were spent, and minds were geared to disciplined repetitiveness. Such minds – of Orwellian dimensions, 'Big-Brother' conditioned – were most often, unable to release themselves from the chains of restricted conformity. Through the ages, poor people have been the component subjects of books, never have they been the authors of them. This view of reality – as I see it anyway – directs an enormous amount of suspicion on the authenticity of history, as we have been told it at our schools, as we have read in our history literature, and more particularly, as we have viewed it in our media, within newspapers, television and radio programmes, cinemas and even as graffiti on walls.

My father – who was a poor worker struggling for subsistence most of the time – was extraordinarily informed about politics and religion. Also in the midst of his political peers, he was comfortably eloquent, more particularly because he was articulate and intelligent. Come to think of it, within the day-to-day wrangles of political power struggles in 1950-60s Britain, he knew more – and he articulated himself better – than the teachers at my school. He reached this stature - with very little time in his life to spare - through wartime experience - which taught a lot of other people a lot of things – and through specifically directed social interactions. Being uneducated – that is to say, not beyond rudimentary educational expertise – he learned of all of the true goings-on of his age, mainly through the 'pure word of mouth grapevine'. This is to say that, after the state taught him elementary literacy, he 'self-developed' discriminatory skills that enabled him to pick the best meat portions out of all of the information that was made available to him, in radio and television news bulletins, in newspapers, and particularly, in many of the public meetings and the social functions that he attended. Because he had never gained opportunities to read books – authored invariably by 'establishment' protagonists – his abilities to see through all of the smoke and all of the mirrors were simplistically lucid. With strong powers of logic he was most often able to assimilate simple facts – about him everywhere – within formed conclusions that were strong and powerful, most of the time, of an anti-establishment nature.

He was not exceptional however. In the Britain of my boyhood, distinct divisions prevailed between those that strived for subsistence – the 'have-nots' – and those that were comfortable – materially with time freedoms - as privileged establishment participants. Many – but not all – of the 'have-nots' most often disputed the truth of available 'official' information – vended in the prevailing media – whereas establishment exponents frequently expressed their disgust of disrespectful insinuations targeted at the integrity of establishment leaders. The 'old boy network' then – as of now – formed a polarised force to retain – and to maintain – its own interests. Of all of the 'have-not' grapevine listeners, most remained very small minded however. While sympathising with their militant peers, they remained indifferent, caring only about their personal possessions and their leisure. As far as they were concerned, they weren't members of deprived groups, they were individuals with particular needs. They would conform and comply with the powers that surrounded them, just as their mothers, their fathers and their grandparents had done, in the midst of widespread destitution if need be, even in the midst of 'grand' wars, with multitudes dying. Yet, during the ages of war, all of the 'have-nots' grapevined vigorously within a single homogenous group. What was certain long before the wars - then and now - was that the information 'super highway' in Britain and in the rest of Europe – as it existed before the Internet – comprised not one, but 'two' distinct broadcasting channels. One was the official 'respectability' channel that was sanctioned and adhered to by all of the conformists, and the other was the 'word-of-mouth grapevine' that engaged itself in the assault of the establishment, denigrating the integrity of its members and its leaders. Since William the Conqueror arrived on English shores, the 'grapevine' has always been the force of the majority of the populace, strong and covertly powerful. Not needing as much acceptance, the establishment's channel is – and always has been - potent also, because traditionally it is two tiered, and thus complicated. It is able – with the support of a judiciary full of 'old school tie' members – to broadcast penaltian threats, and – with military support – reprisal threats, and with a strong central fiscal institution, financial persuasions. Semi-independently within a sub-official channel, religious dictates of all kinds augment the main official channel, with concepts of goodness, orthodoxy for decency and most particularly nowadays – with the Christmas theme pushed vigorously – conscience for generosity.

With the accession of the mad king George 3rd of Britain – elector of the Holy Roman Empire and king of Hanover – who was embroiled most of the time with Europe, its wars and particularly the Seven Years War – formidable change arrived for the minions of England and North America. As the colonials abroad in the America 'to-be' formed a new 'Continental Congress' to utilise Thomas Jefferson's 'Declaration of Independence', Thomas Paine – an English colonial immigrant – was already utilising new printing technology with his Pennsylvania Magazine. In this way – in contrast to the communications scene in Britain – he augmented the prevailing 'grapevine', in the midst of a literate populace. With the bulk of north American immigrants originating from the west of Europe with an English sourced - 'Puritan' biased - majority, strong counter-acting 'Papacy' and dominion 'Regency' influences were absent. Really – through the efforts of people like Paine – the doctrines of 'Republicanism' sprouted in the 'New World' because it could. Papacy influences were greatly diminished within the colonies, because most of the immigration had been sourced from Luther and Calvin 'Puritan' domains in the west of Europe. Also, all of the incumbent 'Royal Dynasties' were primitive savages. Instead of being adhered to, they became fodder for annihilation - in one way or another - just like the buffalo hoards that ranged the plains of Virginia, eventually. This story will not be discussed here however. It is already well told.

Section Eighteen:
American Slaves And British Production:

What was most disturbing then – in the midst of all of the noble aims of Jefferson and Paine – was the expansion of slavery in the north American southern regions, to cultivate and to export 'cotton' on an unprecedented, grand – economically lucrative – scale. In contrast to tobacco - also exported vastly during these times - cotton bonded George 3rd's Britain to north America, economically. Britain's cotton textile manufacturing activities, during the last half of the eighteenth century, increased proportionately with the forceful population of Africans in the south of his American colonies. Land cultivation for food had been the prime expedient of existence for all in Britain, prior to African slavery, even for all of the evolving colonialists that engaged themselves in conquering foreign territories, until 'cotton' arrived on the scene. Then – with its cheap abundance – cottage industries appeared all about – mostly in the north west of England where the climate was favourable for 'cotton' storage – to process it, for economic gain. Profoundly, it was the abundance of raw 'cotton' – obtained from the exploited efforts, and the subsequent misery - of African slaves that drove 'cotton' processors to devise methods and means to deal with all of the cheaply obtained surpluses. Cottage production transformed into 'water-mill house production, and large portions of the agrarian population of Lancashire transformed themselves into cotton hand spinners, and – due to the consequent supply surplus of spun cotton yarn – cotton hand weavers, uplifting their subsistence and ridding themselves of arduous agricultural toil. None of it was enough however. The magnitude of reliable and persistent raw 'cotton' surplus was overwhelming, as was the subsequent demand for the textiles that were produced from it. Inevitably, people like John Kay(inventor of the 'Flying Shuttle-1733'), James Hargreaves(inventor of the 'Spinning Jenny-1770 AD'), Samuel Crompton(inventor of the 'Spinning Mule-1779 AD) and Edmund Cartwright(inventor of the 'Power Loom-1789 AD') engaged themselves in the industrial mayhem of the day, to realise the true potential of the scene, somewhat successfully.

Where one thing invariably leads to another, new production machines in new mills could not be exploited maximally with water power. Inventions within the tin mining industry of Cornwall, evolved successively by Thomas Newcomen(inventor of the 'Steam Engine-1712 AD'), James Watt(inventor of the 'Separate Condenser Steam Engine-1769 AD'), Mathew Boulton(Necomen's associate) and Richard Trevithick(inventor of the first 'Pressurised Steam Engine-1797 AD' and the first 'Steam Locomotive-1801 AD) were utilised in – massively pioneering - textile factories throughout Lancashire and Derbyshire, all complete – and all consuming – by the end of the first quarter of the nineteenth century. Then the whole industrial scene within all of George 3rd's Britain spurted; adopting a new stance, recognised now in all of the pertinent history books that are around, as the 'Industrial Revolution'. Completed – all pervasively – with the early development of railways in Britain, emanating eventually – and massively - in the British 'Indian' colony after they exploded into the whole of Europe and North America. In an ironic sort of way, serfs of the land – everywhere – were circumstantially relieved of toil with the introduction of steam powered machinery into agricultural environments. Conversely – with slavery entrenched throughout the Americas – the seeds of a new style of slavery sprouted with flourishing magnitude in Britain at first, but then throughout the Germanies, even as far as northern Italy 'to-be'. This was the slavery of the factory. The ultimate aberration of the new semi-automated industrial age, where workers in their millions plugged motion gaps - manhandling raw materials and machine produce – within sways of industrial output – in the midst of arrays of automatons. Deprived of their natural environments, these workers – in the throws of 'Mules' and rolling conveyor belts – were 'liberty to live' restricted slaves, with their worth duly exploited within their world of relentless production. A world much pontificated about by Karl Marx and Friedrich Engels, both of whom later expanded the 'grapevine', vastly. Not to be digressed into, at this juncture.

Nowadays, we are able to read in biased history books all about George Stevenson(the inventor of the 'Stevenson's Rocket' locomotive-1829 AD), being persuaded perhaps that he was 'the' great pioneer of steam locomotives in Britain. He was certainly 'a' pioneer, but he was not – as is commonly believed – 'the' man, the original inventor. You see, with the significant evolvement of industrial technology in the textile industry in Britain – with all of the populace re-locating itself, with barges moving all of the raw materials about, and with ships rounding the land - the 'grapevine' became rampant, not only with regard to social and political events, but also in relation to critical technical know-how. Remarkably – and purely circumstantially – critical technical know-how about steam engine locomotion – as distinct from railway locomotion – was acquired by Robert Stevenson(the son of George Stevenson, and the co-inventor of 'Rocket') in Rio de Janeiro, Brazil while he was waiting for a ship to return him to England. There he coincidentally met Richard Trevithick in the year 1829 AD, staying in his hotel, waiting for the same ship. Having spent some time in Peru installing his new steam engines in silver mines to abate flooding, Trevithick was forced to abandon all and run for his life, due to the small matter of a revolution occurring in his Peruvian work region. Apparently he became very unpopular because he facilitated the incumbent dictator, who was soon ousted. Having tramped – in poverty and destitution – from Peru to Rio in Brazil, Trevithick enlightened Stevenson about many technical aspects, later utilised in the 'Rocket' and other subsequent railway locomotives developed soon after the inauguration of the Manchester to Liverpool – arch original – public transport railway line in the year 1832 AD.

Very often, all of the complicated convolutions of historical events and circumstances are over-simplified within 'school tuition' styled history books – written by 'old school tie' boffins – with a view to bolstering the establishment, perversely and untruthfully. Another approach – which is common, especially within the realms of the BBC – is to simply exterminate chunks of information that contradicts promotional themes. With strong representations on behalf of Thomas Edison, the American official propaganda mechanism has managed to place him in a position of prominence - historically speaking - within most available learning media. Yet he was not actually the inventor of the incandescent light bulb, as contended. An Englishman was, named James Swan. Nor was he the architect of electrical power generation in 1920-30s America. This distinction is to be directed towards a Hungarian immigrant to America named Tesla, whose concepts and designs were adopted and incorporated in the first – grand scaled – hydro-electric power station at Niagara Falls in Canada during the early 1930s AD.

Section Nineteen:
The British Empire – Some You Win, Some You Lose

With George 3rd of Britain – later also to become the king of Hanover in the year 1814 AD – and his 'Baron' descendents in Parliament, licking their financial wounds at the end of 'The Seven Years War', exorbitant taxes were levied on American colonials, somewhat detrimental to the 'British Commonwealth' as it turned out. From the year 1773 AD, the formation of opposing armies – inspired and led by George Washington – facilitated the 'American War for Independence' which threatened colonial cotton imports – and tobacco imports - into Britain. In its eventuality, the American independence thing turned out to be a notoriously expensive affair, both in terms of lost manpower within the British colonial army, and in terms of lost economic resources. However, many colonialists loyal to George 3rd moved north into Canada, long settled and stable after the defeat of the French at the battle of Quebec. Even before the commencement of conflicts the British pushed northwards through Canada, up to the St Lawrence river, surveying the landscape diligently and meticulously. In this context, the land lying north of what became the 'lost' American colonies was strongly secured, and a lot of economic infrastucture was established. Certainly, Britain made much good of – what became – a thriving fur trade.

Additionally, before George 3rd's door to American was shut in the year 1776 AD, during his significant explorative voyage in the good ship 'Endeavour'(within the period 1768-71 AD), James Cook discovered additional 'new worlds' far to the east in the Pacific ocean, later developed as part of the British Commonwealth. New Zealand and Australia were subsequently evolved in the new battle for world domination, within which Louis 15th – successor to Louis 16th – influence floundered, and within which the British Commonwealth ascended, even without its American complement. Not just because of new discoveries, but also because of the British subjugation of India, from the Punjab down to the Indian ocean coast, completed with the 'East India Company' solidly founded within fifty years of American expulsion. By 1858 – the year of the start of formal British rule in India – all of the minions of motherland Britain – like it or not – were industrial 'termites', processing vast proportions of the world's resources, generating enormous amounts of wealth. Yet still – even in the wake of the world's largest political upheaval - the French revolution - the barons of old in motherland Britain retained their ancestral territory. What had changed – at that juncture in the mid nineteenth century – was that this territory had become de-populated of minions. All of the incumbents had flocked to the new factories, which they hoped would provide them with a better way of life than that of land serfs, suppressed by barons of old. However, by the time of the 'Peterloo' debacle in the year 1819 AD, they discovered otherwise.

Just to think of it. While great portions of the world were still insular and savage – particularly inner Africa – and other significant portions functioned mostly with 'slavery', Thomas Paine was actively feeding 'the grapevine' in the midst of the 'War for American Independence'. He wrote sixteen crisis papers between 1776-83 AD, many of which were read to 'rebellion troops' by the order of George Washington. Yet again, just a few literates were able to spread news, dictums and commonly acknowledged themes to all of the illiterates, by word of mouth. The source of which was mass produced by means of letterpress printing techniques. In the Europe 'to-be' during this period the ecclesiastic world – in conjunction with all of the political hierarchies – retained a firm grip on written information sources. Prominent Catholics and prominent protestants all about, preached to the illiterate masses, easily and conveniently within the established order of religious worship, within sophisticated – people management – networks, touting grand elaborate buildings dedicated to this purpose. Church attendance on Sundays was in itself then, a religious dictum of universal conformity. Very effectively – still after all of the decades of puritan struggles against the Papacy – the Catholic's version of the grapevine was espoused to individuals through the confession box, with multitudes of priests consolidating anti-contraception themes on a one-to-one basis.

Within Protestant Britain – free of the 'Holy Roman Empire' and of the suppression of a 'sovereign' monarch – Parliament ruled during this period. George 3rd who kept on thrusting for more political influence was rendered impotent by sophisticated 'lawyer styled' politicians like Edmund Burke, active in Parliament at that time. He was the author of clever essays, extolling the virtues of Parliamentarianism. Yet all that he had to say was to do with the retention of old 'baron styled' control of all of the British minions. When Thomas Paine returned from America in the year 1787 AD to write his renowned 'The Rights of Man-1792 AD' - hopefully he thought, to reach the ears of the minions in Britain - he was persecuted for producing seditious 'treason biased' literature by the 'old-boy Parliamentary network', led by Burke. These events – excluding biblical phenomena - amounted to the first battle of the literary magnates in the world, which evolved to nowhere then, but which later inspired 'Das Kapital' – Karl Marx 1894 AD. Long before him however – and before the advent of Paine's philosophy - in stark contrast to the prevailing political scene in Britain during the 1790s decade, the great nation of France - ascended by Louis 13th - was tottering under the rule of Louis 16th. Uncannily, Thomas Paine the persecuted, found refuge in Paris in the year 1792 AD immediately after the long reigning 'Bourbon' dynasty was permanently exterminated with the execution – at the guillotine – of Louis 16th. Similarities between this event and the execution of Charles 1st in England ceased subsequently with the arrest of 300,000 or so people, 17,000 of which were guillotined by the year 1794 AD. In a wilderness of ignorance and tyranny the minions of France – for a long time oppressed, starved and subjugated by the 'Bourbon' dynasty – strived for 'people power', only to discover that their new order was seriously threatened by yet another tyrant. He was the worst deviant of all time; Maxmillian Robespierre.

Section Twenty:
While The French Sorted Themselves Out:

Somehow – for a short while anyway – the 'National Convention' that inspired the original insurrection against Louis 16th prevailed, due to Thomas Paine – an elected member of the 'Convention' during 1792-3 – and due to the legacies of Voltaire and Jean-Jaquas Rousseau. Paine – imprisoned by Robespierre and scheduled for execution just a day before Robespierre himself was condemned and executed – escaped death by a whisker. His jailers mixed up the execution queue on the day, with him omitted. Notably, 'Convention' members – mostly literate and educated – had been influenced by 'Candide', written by Voltaire in the year 1759 AD, and by 'Lettres Philosophique' of the same author, written in the year 1774 AD. Undoubtedly also, they were influenced by 'Social Contract' written by Rousseau in the year 1762 AD, which opened with the sentence: "Man is born free, but everywhere he is in chains" and which also advocated adherence to 'The General Will'. In all probability, for-the-world-to-be, Rousseau also revolutionised the 'Convention's' thinking with 'Emile', written near to those revolutionary times in the year 1788 AD. For-the-world-to-be because 'Emile' dared to delve into the possibility of raising all of the minions – French ones anyway – out of the depths of ignorance through education. Like Paine, Rousseau was forced to leave his mother country(France) for his own safety after writing 'Emile'. Such was the resistance of the clergy and the nobility in the France of Louis 16th. Understandably – with a long, long train of victims and with a lot of baskets full of severed heads – the 'Convention' was truly convulsed, with an urge to rejuvenate the themes of France's great thinkers. In this context, the influential tyrant; Robespierre was be-headed with a very blunt guillotine, without the occurrence of an aftermath. At this conclusion, the guillotine was not re-used much.

Now – as a consequence of the political revolution in France – a great void was established within the mosaic of regencies that constituted Europe 'to-be'. In fact, a serious threat to regents of the likes of George 3rd in Britain – an elector of the Holy Roman Empire – and the Medici dynasty in northern Italy, along with the Papacy, conspicuously complacent in Rome. Of course, the Medici dynasty – in absolute cahoots with the Hapsburgs in Austria and Spain – with sordid expectations, quickly accommodated Austrian troops throughout its territory, particularly northwards of Turin. Yet long before the French 'Convention' managed to quell all of the Robespierre styled death hysteria - not really concluded until the year 1794 AD – the Bourbon regent Charles 4th of Spain, combined his navy with the navy of Britain's George 3rd to support French royalist bastions in the port of Toulon, France in the year 1793 AD. This naval combination was not in any sense the formation of a military coalition between the two nations. It was simply the formation of the 'Holy Roman Empire' – with Bourbon dynasty strengthening - in support of others of its kind, struggling for the restoration of regency rule in France. Importantly at that time, Parliamentarians in Britain could not justify the presence of the British navy – and the Spanish navy – in the port of Toulon, belligerent and spoiling for a war, because France was becoming a republic of the people. Where Parliament in Britain was supposed to be for the people, it was still really for the barons 'of-old', just a puppet of

George 3rd, along with all of the other pseudo parliaments of Europe.

Anyway, Toulon fell to the new republican forces of its homeland, just before which, the British and the Spanish scurried away like rabbits. Meantime, they had sewn the seeds of an enormous – unprecedented – evolvement, which was devoid of religious issues/conflicts. The new republic of France, being forced to quell incumbent pro-regency factions, and being compelled to defend all of its borders – and its coasts – quickly grew into a strong military regime, that was led eventually – and totally – by those that helped most to keep it a 'people's' republic. Gaining favour initially with the successful quelling of rebellions – at the Tuileries Palace against royalist insurgents, and at Toulon – Napoleon Bonaparte ascended militarily, as a principal protector of the new republic. With subsequent intrusions into French territory from the north of Italy by Austrian – Hapsburg – troops during the year 1796 AD, his military stature rose further when he was directed to lead the French republican 'reactionary' invasion of northern Italy, which extended in its eventuality to Rome. At this juncture, Napoleon had successfully dislocated one of the great military arms of the Hapsburgs by defeating its colonial army in Italy, but additionally, the Devici province and the Papacy in the Vatican were engulfed in the sway of republicanism, albeit of a French kind.

Much before he became France's – and really Europe's - first non-regency dictator, Napoleon – with much esteem under his belt – made the case to the new French 'Convention' to attack the European royalist disease at its source; in Austria against the Hapsburgs. He was duly authorised, expediting this task in the year 1797 AD, just as successfully as his conquest of northern Italy. He went further however, extending his exploits into the independent Republic of Venice, ending eleven hundred years of local rule. In accordance with the treaty of Campo Formio, the Austrian 'Hapsburg' dynasty was firmly restrained, being forced to conform to strict directives. Yet the goal that he sought most of all – second perhaps to his desire to become an emperor - was the defeat of Britain, the invasion of which he actually planned in the year 1798 AD, with the conclusion that the British navy in the vicinity of the English Channel was too strong. A very poignant conclusion in the light of subsequent events. Choosing to ignore the British problem – temporarily maybe? – his ambitions outstretched themselves. By masquerading south and east, he considered it possible to conquer his way through to India – via Ottoman territory and Egypt – to join up – with 15,000 of his men - with the Tipu-Sahib revolutionary forces in India, to drive out the British. Remarkably, he succeeded in this objective as far as Alexandria – and as far as the Pyramids – with numerous battle successes that were notable during the period 1798-99. Yet any master plan is easily thwarted with 'a spanner in the works'. With the bugbear of the British navy prevailing, through Horatio Nelson's victory at Abu Qir Bay, near Alexandria – in the battle for the Nile river(1798) - Napoleon was unable to consolidate his supply route, to continue his drive towards India. By this time, he had reached Syria.

To say that Napoleon over extended his resources in the midst of his glorious ambitions, is an under statement, which really – taking his ludicrous invasion of Russia into account, later during the year 1812 AD – amounted to an inevitable tragedy for the French people. Having previously endured destitution and starvation under the rule of the Bourbon Louis's, and after ascending within the control regimes of Napoleon to the status of 'rulers of Europe', all were eventually placed back into a monarchy styled realm until the 2nd republic was founded in the year 1848, under the presidency of Napoleon 3rd. Somewhat ominously, nobody has ever made the case to me that Napoleon Bonaparte was a military – and a political - genius that exhibited extraordinary leadership magnitude throughout his time in power. Utilising the newest weapons technology of the day – canons/explosives – he systematically demolished organised resistance – foreign armies – to his will and his force, with remarkable consistency. Historical evidence suggests that he was specially endowed to lead his armies, with his toughness, his determination and – most of all – his cleverness, particularly in the midst of chaotic military battles. Successive international coalitions formed to combine multiple regency armies to oppose the French republican army, just dissipated in the wake of Napoleonic battles. In all – during Napoleon's ascendancy/descendancy – six such coalitions existed, with Georgian Britain conspicuously in the midst of it all, with each and every formation. From the beginning, subsequent coalition formation evolved due to Britain – characteristically – breaching previous peace agreements. In this context, George 3rd – and his puppet Parliament with Edmund Burke prominent within it – certainly did not want to acquiesce Napoleonic virtues.

In the political context, the evidence of the circumstances leading to Napoleon proclaiming himself 'Emperor' with 'first consul' in the year 1799, suggests that – in the initial instant anyway – he was a reluctant dictator. Faced with an imminent insurrection against the new political executive – the 'Directory of 500' – by just a few with prominence within it, he circumvented to his absolute advantage. Certainly, he didn't instigate matters in this regard. They were evident on his return from Egypt. Concluding perhaps that the 'Directory of 500' was unmanageable – as indeed the coup d'etat exponents had – a golden opportunity for him – as the leader of thousands of armed soldiers – arose, to avoid all of the risks of Thomas Paine's type of philosophy, and to simplify all of the wrangling complexities of republican rule. Whatever, from that juncture a great wave of reform spread about France, relating to education, communication, legalisation and even infrastructure modernisation. Great portions of the city of Paris were demolished to facilitate the construction of grand boulevards, and the 'Napoleonic code' was founded, defining personal rights in relation to property, which in turn – within the boundaries of his dominion, and with the force of his army – virtually eradicated urban criminality and rural banditry. Most importantly perhaps, during his reign, the whole basis of education in France was reformed, from its base levels to its higher echelons, much to facilitate the use of pioneering - nationally distributed – newspapers. In stark contrast to 'Holy Roman Empire' legacies and to the legacies of British monarchs and their accompanying Parliaments, Napoleon Bonaparte stretched his arms to pull his people out of the enormous quagmire of ignorance. With pioneering news media, France's 'grapevine' was much enhanced, with consequent technological and military impetus.

Section Twenty One:
Britain: The Evil State:

Re-focusing on my minion styled existence in this world, my 'state' - I have concluded on numerous occasions - is a 'Buffoon'. Truly a stupid force, riddled with guilt of its legacies, full of noble – and even decent – intentions, but oh so naïve. Phenomenally inept and compulsively prejudiced, most of the time because its 'establishment' is – and always has been – dominated by 'the old school tie brigade', which has always – and still is – riding along on the wave of privilege, educated in elite schools and inevitably affiliated with all others with Christian middle class values. The stupid 'state' that lobotomised my mother, to compound all of the anguish and all of the cruelty that she had endured. The stupid 'state' that allied with my cruel father, to facilitate the continuance of his hegemony style, in the wake of the devastation that he had already caused. The induction of my mother into a mental institution left her children exposed to all of the adversities of that time, because they were a nuisance, particularly to my father – my own kin, but the step father of my siblings – but also to all others obliged towards the alleviation of suffering. With father adopting a complete 'ditch them' attitude, these alleviators were my mother's mother and my mother's married siblings, who agreed in the midst of the initial aftermath to adopt my half siblings and me singularly, sharing us between their households. Then – being the youngest – I remember being placed in the middle of a circle formed by them all, and being asked as to who I would like to live with. Well I can tell you with certainty, that this strategy – regardless of how well meaning it was – fostered even more disaster. As if there hadn't been enough.

You see, the roots of the conflicts that arose were buried in the hearts of the spouses of my mother's siblings, who at that time, were young with their own desires of motherhood – not yet experienced – at that juncture. Expelled into an improvised camping bed every day straight after school – just about five years old – I was an unloved banished soul, actually persecuted by a so called virtuous God loving Jehovah's Witness, with a very mean streak in her personality, born of resentment. At that early age, I learned that badness was nothing to do with professed religious affiliations, and that many – if not the most – of those that were bad, concealed themselves behind pseudo 'goodness' cloaks. Anyway, my mother's brother Peter, who later acquired a fortune in New Zealand – my new guardian and the spouse of my persecutor – fathomed the situation before the fringes of cruelty were reached. I was told to sit in his motorcycle side car and wait. I waited, and I waited, and then I became bored with waiting. On my return to the household, the last piece of porcelain that that couple possessed was being used to fragment the mirror over the fireplace, in their lounge. All of the other crockery that they possessed between them had preceded this, descending to fragmented uselessness all about the place. Certainly, my happiness was not to be found within the realms of my extended family. Moreso, because on my return to my grandmother's house, I was sexually assaulted by one of my other uncles, who I had to share a bed with in my grandmother's bathroom. Grandmother – the matriarch of Jehovah's Witnesses in Llandaff, Cardiff at the time – was blissfully unaware of her son's evil, but later, when my half sibling John subsequently complained about similar molestations, she chose to remain in denial about the true nature of her son. Such is the power of protection compulsions in mothers.

Grandmother did however, act to protect me also, on hearing that my father sought my return to his guardianship. Knowing all about – or at least something about – his legacy, she duly placed me in an isolated farm near to Builth Wells with another of my mother's brothers, Tony and his wife. These were wonderful people and their farm was heaven for me, but all was short lived, due to my father, and due to the 'ignorant', 'stupid' state. Happy times elapsed when father came strutting to the farm gate - when my uncle was absent - with the local police constable, to collect me. To correct my illegal abduction, as it was portrayed. In the eyes of the policeman – who dined us both just prior to us vacating back to Blackpool – father was the caring soul that had been wronged. All of the time he was jovial. He was also blinded with the prejudice of his orthodox vision, because he failed to see – let alone recognise – the anguish on my face, which persisted for a long time afterwards. In the meantime, the old council house in Blackpool had fallen by the wayside, replaced with a newer, smaller one to accommodate just the two of us, situated nearby on the same council housing estate. It was a few years before I fathomed the true cause of all of those consequences, much after I reached my mid-twenties age, in fact. With strong parallels of Georgian children in Britain, who were exploited in the factories, just to – primarily – supplement the incomes of their parents, in the new 'Socialist' Britain of my age, I was reclaimed legally and expeditiously by my father – with the support of the state, naively – to enable him to live as a single person in cheap – state subsidised – housing, as he had previously with a whole family. He could not have done this without me. This was truly his motive for his reclamation of me, corroborated by his neglect of me from that juncture onwards, and by subsequent cruelty that evolved when he eventually got to co-habit with his co-adulterer.

For a while however, this person chose to lead a clandestine lifestyle in order to stem the swell of poison pen letters that were about the same council housing estate, originated from the watching neighbours of my mother's demise. Strangely, the embedded instincts within me – all of the wild ones within us all, deep down – came to the fore during that period, to the extent that I became almost feral, left alone to run wild, exuberant with my own confidence, which grew beyond realistic management at times. Since, I have possessed strong steaks of self reliance and independence - causing numerous difficulties for me during my term in the military - but which since, have successfully propelled me through various challenges and difficulties. From all that I can remember about my father, he was most distinctly an atheist, not a deist or an agnostic. My contentions about his atheism are based on his total disbelief of the existence of anything spiritual. Due maybe to his lack of education? Yet enclaved in the security of all of his brothers as a child, he was never really threatened by anything. Ironically, within the conciliatory atmosphere of post WW2 Britain, he was supported, while he threatened others, like my eldest half brother who paid a heavy price for his 'bed wetting' affliction under his umbrella. He died at the age of forty two years, deranged, just like his mother – who was also my mother – before him.

Section Twenty Two:
Anything To Rid Europe Of Napoleon Bonaparte

Napoleon Bonaparte – 'the cruellest dictator of all time', according to the British propaganda of his day - from all of the information that I have managed to gather about him, was quite a different kind of man to my father. Such propaganda – characteristic of the governing 'hoodwinkers' of that era – was devised to conceal a political situation – lasting through seventeen years of European warfare – of a completely opposite nature. In the true context, Napoleon Bonaparte was the good guy of the age, and George 3rd – with his crony Parliament – was the real villain. While 'Boney' – so named derogatively by the British – extended the initial revolution in France into fundamental life concepts, Lord Walpole(George 3rd's puppet), succeeded by William Pitt, repetitively agitated for war with France, inspiring the 1st coalition, then the 2nd coalition, and then the 3rd coalition and so on, in turn repeated by their successors to the 6th coalition, with Britain being a party to all. Think of this, while Napoleon Bonaparte was working for religious tolerance within Europe, Pitt(the younger) was acting to send the first batch of criminalised deportees to the new lands of New South Wales, which had only just been discovered by Captain James Cook, just a decade or so beforehand.

Here lies the subsequent plot: where Boney was launching new newspapers for his military and his people, the British establishment was getting rid of – permanently - rebellious voices as quick as it could(to penal colonies in New South Wales, Australia in the year 1788 AD). With ignorance/illiteracy prevailing – by enforcement and by neglect - in Britain at that time, the 'grapevine' – which told of better things over the sea – was effectively nullified by this means. Additionally, in Pitt's Britain by the year 1799, it became illegal to consult with co-workers about raising wages, the penalty for which was deportation to New South Wales(Combination acts, later evolving into the Tolpuddle Martyrs controversy). Contrastingly, with the creation of Boney's new 'Continental System', serfdom was abolished, property rights were established in law, measurements – distances, weights etc – were altered to the original 'metric' form, and religious tolerance was extended, within all of the lands subsequently ruled. Even French money measurement was altered, with the introduction of one hundred cents to the franc; simple denary counting. Particularly – as the Napoleonic wars progressed – a large portion of the populace of the Germanies benefited from Napoleon's invasion of their lands. He introduced new laws – with the will of his army to enforce them properly – to protect Protestants where Catholics dominated, and to protect Catholics where Protestants dominated. Much more significantly, all of the Jews within his domains enjoyed equal status, regardless of their nationality. He repealed laws that restricted them to 'ghetto' residences, and he promoted the retention of their rights to own property, to worship and to hopefully pursue careers of their preference. All of this sort of thing culminated soon after the peace of Campo Formio in the year 1797. Like a clever magician, after quelling the manic empires of the Hapsburgs, the Medici's and the Papacy in Italy, Bonaparte despatched his army over to the source of all of the problems, through the Germanies to the Hapsburg dynasty in Austria, to quell that too, and he succeeded. Meanwhile in Britain, in Austria, in Russia and in

Hungary, all of the dynasties – infinitely entwined with the Hapsburgs – sat there fretting. The proof of their collusiveness to control their minions – 'of-old' – was displayed through their willingness – and their eagerness – to form military coalitions between themselves in opposition to Boney.

In all, Napoleon Bonaparte's rule over virtually all of Europe was a volatile one, not least because of king George 3rd of Britain, with his affiliations to the Hapsburg dynasty within the spiritual and the physical elements of the 'Holy Roman Empire'. While invoking massive infrastructure improvements in his motherland – road and sewage systems – and all sorts of new codes – such as a universal tax system and 'The Legion of Honour' meritous military convention – Boney was simultaneously engaged in the suppression of 'Holy Roman Empire' belligerence. The British persistently colluded with the Austrians and the Russians - and of course the Prussians - to assemble armies to attack the French – to restore the ominous Bourbons to power. Any sort of 'skulduggery' method was deemed suitable. Assassination attempts, insurrections and invasions directly into France, all emanating from George 3rd and William Pitt, operating outside of Bonaparte's domain, remaining somewhat impervious. Additionally, the Hapsburgs, by the year 1800 AD flouted the peace of Campo Formio by inspiring a resurgence of their claims to the territory of northern Italy. All were conceded to France again however, in the revised peace treaty of Luneville in the year 1801 AD, after Napoleon's victories over Austrian troops at the northern Marengo plains, Italy and at Hohenlinden, Austria. Yet all was not done. Francis 1st's accession as the first Emperor of Austria – also emperor of the 'Holy Roman Empire', of the house of Hapsburg –

in 1804, re-founded opposition to Napoleon. Yet again, the British had managed to form a coalition with the Russians – or rather, George 3rd and William Pitt through Hapsburg collaborations, had managed to get into 'cahoots' with Alexanda 1st of Russia. Francis – with a smaller army than Napoleon's – invaded the Germanies in Bavaria, with the assumption that the Russians would arrive on the scene, to complement his forces in opposition to Boney. All of which did not actually occur. Napoleon's army intervened and quelled Francis's army before Alexanda's army reached the battle scene at Ulm.

Then, France's 'First Consul' – Napoleon Bonaparte the dictator – excelled, with all of his army fighting heroically, maybe because he had successfully hoodwinked them with his newly founded newspapers. Whatever? From Ulm in the Germanies, the French republican 68,000 strong army – with clever military strategies – defeated the 90,000 strong combined armies of Austria and Russia at Austerlitz in the year 1805 AD. With this victory of 'The Battle of the Three Emperors' – as it became known – all of the minions within Boney's conquered domains benefited, in relation to their subsistence – with many taxes revised or removed – and their religions, and their day-to-day amenities, which were broadly improved. Yet, with all of the chaos all about – with volatile civil scenes everywhere – the French economy did not develop in the same fashion, as that of Britain. All was to do with the strength of the British navy. Only forty two days separated Horatio Nelson's second sea victory – at the battle of Trafalgar – and Boney's conquest of the three emperors at Austerlitz. As much as Bonaparte wanted to invade Britain to put an end to all of its agitations, he was unable, due to the superiority of its navy. The sea battle of Trafalgar confirmed this. Conversely, as much as the George 3rd/Pitt team wanted to restore the Bourbons to the palace of Versailles, they were unable, due to the superiority of Boney's army. The land battle of Austerlitz also confirmed this. Stale mate, so to speak.

In the meantime, Britain, the European isolate, ruled the seas. All of the important ones that facilitated the shipment of important resources from Britain's growing 'Commonwealth', anyway. Cotton for industrial processing, tobacco, tea, sugar, exotic fruits and spices, all supplementing rich fish harvests from home waters and an expanded sheep rearing industry, facilitated particularly by the depopulation of the Scottish highlands. To all of the minions of Britain, Napoleon Bonaparte was a little weedy man with a great big ego, always dressed in the military regalia of the famous French 'Chasseur à Cheval', with an enormous bicorn hat, and always with one hand placed in his waistcoat pocket, posing eagerly. Even a nursery rhyme was prevalent then, known as the 'bogeyman', warning children that Napoleon ravenously ate naughty people: "The Bogeyman will get you". The British press of the day promoted such darogadation, with false claims about Boney's height. 'Little men feel inferior, and must therefore inflate their egos to compensate' was a claim used to authenticate a continuous train of personality focused attacks in the news sheets and the newspapers of the day. However, due to heavy taxes on newspapers – three pence by the year 1802 AD, which was increased to four pence by the year 1815 AD – 'Tory' styled – for the rich – news was exclusive. Nothing of substance ever reached the ears of all of the poor minions of Britain, other than this sort of innuendo, occasionally augmented by the 'grapevine' voice of British naval sailors, with their tales of Horatio Nelson's great sea battles. Then of course, all of this definitive George 3rd styled propaganda was compounded into the enormous visual spectacle of Nelson's column/statue, built in the heart of London. The glorification of it all was expounded in the midst of dramatic changes to London's infrastructure, within the newly created Trafalgar Square. Contrastingly, the French newspapers of the time – such as the 'Moniteur' – were free of tax. By way of compensating for illiteracy, their contents were regularly read aloud in the taverns of Paris, and everywhere else about the land.

Section Twenty Three:
War Economics

At the time of these events, the process of industrialisation in Britain had progressed in advance of France, from the mid 1750s – or so – onwards. The British industrial scene progressed in a Laisse-Faire fashion, unrestricted and uninterrupted because of the absence of war in the homeland, and because the rulers of the day – of the George 3rd and Pitt(the younger) kind – were more interested in taxes and regency, than infrastructure, other than their own regal palaces of course. The British 'Parliament' of the day up to the 'Peterloo' juncture - at the very least - was mostly populated by the land owners, some of whom were powerful and influential. Contrastingly in France from the year 1789 – the year that the Bastille was stormed – all land ownership rights were revised, mostly to the benefit of land serfs. Subsequently – under Bonaparte's rule, serfdom was abolished altogether. In this context, serfs in Britain – of which there were many at the start of the eighteenth century – were more inclined to join the industrial process, augmenting its growth as the century evolved. Then child birth became popular with industrial workers, to augment their subsistence within large family entities. With subsequent increases in population, food demands increased proportionately. Similar events occurred in France – time lagged thirty to fifty years behind Britain - but also, not to the same extent until the close of the century. By the year 1780 AD, 20,000 textile mills existed in Britain to France's 900. By the year 1850 AD, 10,500 kilometres of railway track was laid in Britain, to France's 3,000 kilometres. Contrastingly, France remained agriculturally based for longer because the quality of life for land workers was better, and because a substantial network of old Roman roads existed, better kept than British equivalents. As a result of these changes, Britain's agricultural lands were enclosed to increase the output of food produce, and to facilitate larger scaled livestock farming operations, with fewer farms owned by bigger land owners.

By contrast, throughout Britain with all of the rich gentry pursuing their own self-interest, an Adam Smith styled conglomerate evolved, free of the financial burdens of warfare. In Europe, Napoleon 'commanded' wealth generation activities, inevitably entwined in the quagmire of warfare – at times – on several fronts. From a position of relative impunity, the British agitated for war with France to preserve and to promote 'gentry' enterprises, whereas, Napoleon – who was in every sense, France - waged war in a reactionary fashion, aided with the resources of his minions. Over stretching these resources when the true intentions of Alexandra 1st became apparent – when yet again, he coalesced with the Austrian

Hapsburgs and the British – he invaded Russia in the year 1812 AD, drastically. In this endeavour - and in all of the subsequent endeavours – during his military withdrawal from Russia and during the ominous battle of Leipzig in the year 1813 AD, Boney depleted his prime resource – many of his fit young men – while new factory capitalists in Britain accumulated vast wealth, by means of slave cultivated cotton, and by means of enslaved cotton processors – largely comprising very poorly paid young men, young women and children - in their factories. Interestingly, serfs remained prevalent throughout all of the lands not controlled by Boney, particularly throughout Russia.

With a sort of sub-conscious awareness of the factory scene in Britain, my own life has been shaped by it in an indirect way. I remember alighting to the top deck of a double-decker bus in Blackpool when I was a boy – about ten years old – to see my other grandmother – my father's mother – sitting, at the front - gabbling and pontificating - with a number of her work mates, all 'Woodbine' puffing, as if fresh air was to be avoided like poison. Sat at the back, I viewed it all without her being aware of my presence. There she was, with her towel wrapped around her head – as they used to do everywhere in the Britain of the 1950s – leading her usual avalanche of gossip about anything and everything of non-substance, in the midst of a great smoke cloud, which, when it reached me, was marvellously – almost stuporfyingly – toxic. The oh! so sweet smell of tobacco that intoxicated nearly all of the British working minions. Not just for decades, but for centuries. What a contrast to my other – pious, caring but bigoted – grandmother. It was simple to realise why my father had turned out to be such a puritanical tyrant, in absolute opposition to the legacy of his mother. She was a happy go-lucky uninhibited, untethered, unrepentant campaigner for perversion. Of my father's brothers, not all were from the same father. My father's brother Jack(good old uncle Jack) told me that his mother – the woman at the front of the bus – lived apart from him and his fold of brothers most of the time, mostly away at work in the factory, or moreso in the evenings – in the public houses of Blackpool, drinking, debauching and doing whatever else comes naturally within those sorts of environments. She – and good old grandad, who was still tagging along at that time - originated from Burnley, but inevitably, due to grandmother's priorities in life, Blackpool was a much more attractive place to live.

During my last days at school – which were particularly volatile and dangerous – when I was reviewing options, factories to me were monkey jungle domains, full of my grandmother's kind. I didn't hate the people within them; they were often kind and considerate in their own peculiar way. In fact, compassion is one of their strengths. Often pleasant and unobtrusive, they were most often, willing to listen because they really cared. How on earth did my father turn out like he did? The political mastermind, unwilling most of the time to communicate at grass roots level. Contrastingly, granny was a dear, really. However, to me then – and still now – factories meant routine and monotony. Biking through traffic twice a day with a thermos flask and sandwiches in a rucksack, wishing the days away, just to splash and venture into raucous nights. Brain numb and mentally wasted with monotony and routine, this is how most of those that I went to school with, ended up. When I was a teenager, most of those not well educated found themselves perpetuating the legacy of their forefathers, on shop floors, in factories, foundries, shipyards, or in mines, trains, buses; all as hourly paid workers. After watching that pioneering cinema film of the 1960s: 'Saturday Night, Sunday Morning-Albert Finney', none of it was going to be for me. The 'grapevine' – clearly broadcasted in Finney's film – was my salvation. It confirmed my suspicions about all of the official blurb of the establishment, attempting to lead me into Armageddon. Soon afterwards I still found myself being dragged into the prevailing quagmire, along with most others of my class.

Fortunately, I escaped into the Royal Air Force in the October of the year 1962 AD, before I became totally engulfed. Some years later I found myself in a heavy drop parachute packing factory at Upper Heyford in Oxfordshire. There I completed a lot of hard gruelling work, mostly packing sixty six foot cluster parachutes for army tank drops. After forty eight years or so since that time, I still have hard pads on my little fingers, resulting from the work that I completed then. It took me a while – about a year – to escape from that factory, even with a lot of determination to do so. Happily, I exchanged with somebody at RAF Valley, Anglesey. He could have 'the factory' and all of the urban paraphernalia that went with it. I had had enough of it all during my childhood. On arriving at Valley I was back in the wild of rural Wales, beautiful and enigmatic, tasting just as sweet as it had tasted beforehand when I was in Builth Wells. By contrast, RAF Valley was a very challenging technological environment, with lots of excitement all about during the day-to-day activities of the Air Force's No4 School of Advanced Flying Training, flying Folland Gnats, tentatively and precariously then. Emergency ejections galore and lots of joy rides, sixty thousand feet up in the stratosphere. I was not a slave of my ancestry; I escaped 'the factory', never having to endure its monotony or its repetition since. The 'factory' was never for me. However, I can understand how many of my contemporaries were swallowed up in the industrial turmoil of Britain, just as their ancestors were entrapped, enslaved and consequently stuporfied in the centuries that preceded the 1960s.

Section Twenty Four:
With Bonaparte Gone, The Revival Of Holiness

With his military forces truly spent, and with a whole range of allied belligerents invading France, the great Napoleon Bonaparte – France's first consul – abdicated, escaping to the island of Elba – not very far from his Corsican homeland - in the year 1814 AD. Yet, he was not finished at that juncture, nor was he safe on Elba. After spending three hundred days improving the living conditions of Elbans, he returned with his personal bodyguard of six hundred to Paris, re-recruiting the whole of his previously defeated army as he did so. In the meantime, the coalition allies had restored the Bourbon dynasty with the regent of Louis 17th, Louis 18th. Louis 17th at that time was thought to have died in the Bastille in the wake of the French revolution in the year 1792, but DNA tests conducted in the year 2,000 AD have since proved that the dead prisoner was actually the son of Louis 14th. No information is available about the actual destiny of Louis 17th. The destiny of Louis 18th soon after his placement was clear however. Hardly warm and comfortable on his new throne, he was forced to vacate France as quick as he could, as Napoleon marched back into Paris, followed by his army. Meanwhile, Arthur Wellesley

– newly promoted to: 'The 1st Duke of Wellington' - gathered the allied armies for the big fight, that would decide things permanently: 'The Battle of Waterloo' in the year 1815 AD, fought on Belgian 'to-be' soil, and of which Bonaparte was defeated and captured.

With Napoleon's inevitable banishment to the island of St Helena in the mid Atlantic ocean – miles from anywhere in the world - and with Louis 18th yet again placed on the French throne, 'The Holy Roman Empire' – in total contradiction to what most contemporary historians state – experienced a renowned renaissance. The contention was that 'The Holy Roman Empire' dissolved with the abdication of Francis 1st of Austria – also of the Hapsburg dynasty, and also emperor of 'The Holy Roman Empire' – at the conclusion of the battle of Austerlitz in the year 1806 AD. Before the year of the battle of Waterloo was out however, Francis 1st of Austria and Alexander 1st, the Tsar of Russia – along with the freshly powerful Frederick William 1st(later, Keiser Wilhelm 1st of Germany, in the year 1815 AD) formed 'The Holy Alliance' which avowed to "promote the influence of Christian principles in the affairs of nations", namely the principles of the 'Papacy' in Rome, which just happened at that time to own between 50% and 65% of the agricultural pauper lands of the 'Two Sicilies': the island of Sicily and all of the lands south of Rome, not previously controlled by Napoleon. Much before and much after the formation of the 'Holy Alliance', people starved in these vicinities without much 'Papacy' alleviation. The secret society of the 'Carbonari' – a strong revolutionary political group – was born during the immediate post 'Holy Alliance' years, ascending in power up to the year 1820 AD, just preceding Napoleon's death in the year 1821 AD. More or less when a mammoth French styled revolution was successfully suppressed in the two Sicilies by the combined efforts of king Ferdinand 1st and Pope Pius 7th – with the assistance of Austrian Hapsburg troops – Napoleon Bonaparte was being poisoned to death with arsenic, by his British captors. Carbonari activities in the two Sicilies were in all probabilities, the least of the problems of the people of Naples and its surrounding pauper lands. Here at that time, the 'Mafia' was born, which later migrated with thousands of other destitutes – big time – into the growing cities of the United States of America. Accusations about Napoleon being arsenic poisoned were formed from preceding pathological evidence, some years after his death.

Yet think of this, at the time of Carbonari activities, the legacy of Joachim-Napoléon Murat – king of Naples(1808-1815) and the brother-in-law of Bonaparte – was still fresh. Of Corsican – near Italian descent – Napoleon Bonaparte potentially, could have escaped yet again, to re-launch himself yet again in the region of the two Sicilies, which was rife with dissent and revolution, at least until 1861.
In the meantime, Arthur Wellesley(the Duke of Wellington) acquired fame and rose to prominence, enormously. Really, beyond reasonable proportion, becoming the prime minister of Britain by the year 1828 AD. When all was said and done, he had managed to defeat Napoleon Bonaparte 'once' – with the help of the Prussian army – whereas, Napoleon's forces had conquered nearly the whole of Europe for seventeen years contiguously. Just imagine how the monarchy in Britain spurred its propaganda machine, characteristically over glorifying Wellesley's victory. Bolstering his personality, his

virtues and his pseudo bravery with distinct recognition. Duly elevating him to the higher echelons of British society, and thus paving his way to prominence in Parliament, as the leading minister. Thus, the 'old school tie brigade' was the architect of his collusion – absolutely – with George 4th, who at that time was the regent of his manically mad father, George 3rd. Just imagine it. All of the minions of Britain – not within the ring of glory – should know their place, according to the mad old king – still an elector of the 'Holy Roman Empire' – and the 'Grand Duke', still fired with his victory. Even in the wake of the Perterloo massacre by the year 1820 AD, Britain was still a country – constitutionally speaking – with a prominent monarchy, with glorious armed forces poised to keep it that way, with its Parliament duly subordinated. Yet before the decade expired, with Arthur Wellesley ascending to Prime Minister in the year 1828 AD, a wave of smouldering rebellion evolved, throughout the nation and within Parliament, of which, the likes of Wellesley could not repel. He was forced to resign his government in the year 1830 AD.

Section Twenty Five:
Quell The Rebellion - Again

Within months of Wellesley's resignation, coal miners in Merthyr Tydfil, Wales – who were sustaining wage cuts to the point of starving – congregated in the streets and raided the local 'Debtor's Court', destroying debt records. Then they toured all of the local coal mines and persuaded most other miners to join their protest. In response, Lord Melbourne's new government sent a contingent of the Argyle and Sutherland Highlanders to quell the mob, which in the event, turned out to be too large to control. When some of their weapons were seized, the troops were ordered to fire on the crowd, resulting in a lot of serious injuries and some deaths. Eventually, this uprising was quelled, but not quite to the satisfaction of Lord Melbourne. Quoting records of this incident:

"By 7 June the authorities had regained control of the town through force. Twenty-six people were arrested and put on trial for taking part in the revolt. Several were sentenced to terms of imprisonment, others sentenced to penal transportation to Australia, and two were sentenced to death by hanging – Lewsyn yr Heliwr (also known as Lewis Lewis) for robbery and Dic Penderyn (also known as Richard Lewis) for stabbing a soldier (Private Donald Black of the Highland Regiment) in the leg with a seized bayonet."

"Lewsyn yr Heliwr had his sentence downgraded to a life sentence and penal transportation to Australia when one of the police officers who had tried to disperse the crowd testified that he had tried to shield him from the rioters. He was transported aboard the vessel John in 1832 and died 6 September 1847 in Port Macquarie."

"Following this reprieve the British government, led by Lord Melbourne, was determined that at least one rebel should die as an example of what happened to rebels. The people of Merthyr Tydfil were convinced that Dic Penderyn, a 23-year-old miner, was not responsible for the stabbing, and 11,000 signed a petition demanding his release. The government refused, and Penderyn was hanged at Cardiff market on August 13, 1831. In 1874 it was discovered that another man named Ianto Parker, not Dic Penderyn, had stabbed Donald Black and then fled to America fearing capture by the authorities, and also that rebuttal witness James Abbott, who had testified at

Penderyn's trial, admitted that he had lied under oath, under the orders of Lord Melbourne, in order to secure a conviction."

Just preceding these events, in France, Louis 18th – who remained intransigent about his exclusive royal status - was forced to abdicate in the same year. His replacement - Charles 10th – could rule only within the terms of a new form of constitutional democracy, somewhat aligned with the legacy of the revolution. Similarly in Britain – especially in the wake of the Merthyr Tidfil uprising - faced with a new constitutionally inspired government, the coincidental new monarch – William 4th, son of George 3rd and brother of George 4th – ascended in the face of a new Parliamentary biased constitution, invoked and solidified with the passing of the 'Reform act of 1832'.

Section Twenty Six:
A Remarkable Coup For The European Aristocracy

Yet, all of the minions of both of these countries, largely remained unrepresented. This was particularly so in Britain, because the 1832 reform act only gave a say in the affairs of the nation, to those that owned property, of the male gender. In reality, this did not – at that time – relate to many people at all. Most certainly though at this juncture, in both nations, 'Monarchy' became 'Puppets'. Yet, in the midst of Europe then, the Papacy and the Hapsburg dynasty remained all pervasively powerful. Contrastingly, the Germanies at this juncture - with the ascendancy of Prussian power – remained disunited. Without the reconciliation of religious and regal differences in these lands, the nation of Germany was yet to be born. Likewise, the lands of the Medici dynasty and the two Sicilies. Italy at this juncture, did not exist. Think of this: neither existed by the time that Britain had colonised Australia, New Zealand, a whole string of Polynesian islands in the Pacific, Canada, Cape Colony in the South Africa to be, Jamaica, Trinidad and virtually the whole of India, with just the formality of making 'Queen Victoria' the 'Empress of India' to complete. Remarkably – and somewhat devastatingly as it turned out – absolute monarchy styled 'Belgium' sprang out of the southern regions of 'The Nederland' in the year 1830 AD, in the midst of all of the constitutional changes in Britain and France. As a neighbour of the newly constituted France – which had been distinctively influenced by Napoleon Bonaparte – the new Belgian subjects of Leopold 1st – the first monarch of new Belgium - turned out to be idolists of the old 'The Holy Roman Empire'. Leopold, a Bavarian of the Saxe-Coburg and Gotha heritage had already married – and was a widow of – Princess Charlotte of Wales, the only legitimate child of George 4th of Britain. Besides being created a British Field Marshal and a 'Knight of the Garter', he had already been bestowed the British title of 'his royal highness' by order in council. If you think that Prince Albert enjoyed regency as Queen Victoria's spouse just circumstantially, then consider this: if Princess Charlotte had not died during child birth, she would have ascended to the British throne, and Leopold would have enjoyed equivalent regency status, anyway.

Most certainly – by the evidence of the accession of Leopold 1st – 'The Holy Roman Empire' had not been dissolved in the year 1806 AD – contended by most historical scholars - as a consequence of the abdication of Francis 1st of Austria. By the confirmations of the 'Holy Alliance' founded in 1815, 'The Holy Roman Empire' was alive and kicking long afterwards, certainly by the year 1831 AD. In the midst of all of this, the assertion is made here, that Leopold 1st – who had previously refused monarchical status in the newly formed state of Greece – was just 'matter-of-factly' invited to take total control of the new Belgian lands. Inevitably, in the minds of normal thinkers the question arises: Why should a Bavarian born regent of the Germanies – of Saxe-Coburg and Gotha regency heritage – become the exclusive – all powerful – monarch of a Dutch/catholic decadency? The answer is definitely, that William 4th of Britain – and later, queen Victoria – was in cahoots with the house of Saxe-Coburg and Gotha, the Hapsburgs, the Devicis', the Russian Tsar, Nicholas 1st, Wilhelm 3rd of Prussia and all of the other inter-related affiliates of the not-so-defunct 'Holy Roman Empire', closely bonded still, to the Papacy in Rome. Thus, intricately inter-twined with all of the upheaval and all of the destitution in the two Sicilies, which sewed the seeds of a later revolution of Italy 'to-be'. In accordance with subsequent events, the accession of Leopold 1st turned out to be a catastrophe for the whole world by the 1870s decade. With his son Leopold 2nd duly inheriting his throne, Laizze Faire styled European adventurism evolved into international megalomania, far beyond the fears – or perhaps the nightmares? – of Napoleon Bonaparte. Such adventurism, given birth by queen Elizabeth 1st and Francis Drake – but later brilliantly exploited by Dutch protestants - in the main, delved and prodded the east of the world in search of precious substances/produce, to enhance the subsistence of multiplying populaces. Such produce then, was worth more than all of the gold – quite literally – of the prevailing Spanish empire.

Section Twenty Seven:
The Control Of Foreign Minions

At the start of it all, exotic spices originating from the Chinese/Mongolian provinces reached Europe precariously and intermittently via land routes, in all, very long land routes forming 'The Silk Road', traversing virtually the whole of the eastern and the middle eastern continents, to Europe. Multiples of successive merchants – each taking a slice of profit for themselves – formed a linked supply chain of exotic – exorbitantly priced – 'seeds of desire', consumed only by the elite of European societies. Thus creating an enormous impetus for masters of the World's oceans to explore for alternatives. Duly discovered by the Portuguese long before Dutch, Spanish and British ascendancy. Then successively by the Dutch and the British, even in the midst of Spanish prominence in the west of the world. Dutch colonies – in addition to 'New Holland' in the west, which later became 'New York' – were established on the southern tip of Africa – Cape Colony – and in the eastern apologues of Indonesia, much before British mariners ventured that way. In fact, much before, with sufficient time to establish the Dutch East India Company, which for a time, riveted the world outside of 'The Dutch Federation', with 'trade' power, and with consequent political force. All while 'The Dutch Federation' struggled – continuously - for independence from the Spanish Hapsburgs. After the gentry of Britain cottoned-on to what was really going on, British/Dutch rivalry was immense, on the seas and all about the orient. Politically stronger than 'The Dutch Federation' – free of Hapsburg, Devici and Papacy thrusts – British nobility financed maritime adventures that were really fairly safe bets, based on legends about

Dutch success. Not at all satisfied with their own discovery of new resources around the initial Dutch international dominions, the British established their own East Indies Company – growing all about the world relentlessly - to impinge on Dutch international interests. Likewise the French, with much less success.

By the time Napoleon Bonaparte ventured into Egypt and Syria, the East India Company – formed by the British 'filthy-rich' fraternity, many of whom were inherent English land owners – were recruiting, training and despatching mercenaries – big time – into the northern Punjab region of India 'to-be' – and extensively southwards from there – to establish and to protect new trading environs, created principally to supply 'exotica' – Britain's equivalent to Spain's 'Elderado' – to the British elite of the day. Ultimately, to those that could boost the share premiums of East India Company investors. With cunning subtlety, while the worthless underlings of India 'to-be' were militarily oppressed and enslaved, the provincial Maharaja rulers were enticed, bribed and even venerated, to acquiesce the new British wealth creation quest – born during George 3rd's reign – in opposition to the welfare and the wellbeing of their own people. The real basis of the whole plot – besides the obvious activity of enslavement to generate money making resources - was however, the recruitment, the subversion and the indoctrination of local underlings, to build formidable armies at source, led by British mercenary officers. In this way, the framework of the enormous East India Company enterprise in India 'to-be' was consolidated, well beyond sensible contraction. Yet at times, this was a very precarious strategy to pursue. Just twenty years preceding queen Victoria's ascendancy as 'The Empress of India' the indigenous troops of 'The East India Company' mutinied in the year 1856 AD, to support the troops of the Nawab of Bengal. Not particularly influenced by British enticements, the Nawab stormed Fort William in Calcutta to restrain military expansion. The notorious 'Black Hole of Calcutta' incident occurred at this time, along with the siege of 'Lucknow' in the year 1857 AD. All of which inspired the British government to cede the political power of 'The East Indies Company' in India. Never mind all of the poppycock you have heard about Muslim soldiers not wanting to handle rifle cartridges manufactured from the fat of pigs. This probably occurred as recorded, but it was not the prime cause of the mutiny.

Meanwhile – with the Nawab and his supporters duly subdued, the company gave birth to a new cotton belt to supplement the American supply source, and new – extensive - tea plantations. All of which were supplemented somewhat ominously with new 'Poppy' plantations. An appreciation of the enormity of these events is not possible without a true perspective view of the number of people that were involved, in the midst of the huge land mass of India 'to-be', with all of its hungry minions, of which, even then, there were multitudes of millions in number. Not only did the produce of the poppy plantations – Opium – end up being shipped – big-time – to China during 'The East India Company's' late days, it was also shipped after queen Victoria was made the 'Empress of India' and after the British 'Raj' was established, to replace the military infrastructure of 'The East India Company'. By implication, the British nation was complicit in illegal drug smuggling into China. All because those directly complicit, did not much want to purchase Chinese tea with silver coins, as was required in law there.

With the increasing drug addiction of Chinese incumbents, bartering opium for tea was a much more lucrative alternative. Worse, when hostilities broke out between the Chinese authorities and the opium traders – supported with mercenary troops – the British government adopted 'gunboat diplomacy', reinforcing the invading military in the year 1839 AD. Just to add insult to injury, the Chinese province of Hong Kong was also annexed by British military forces soon afterwards.

Of all of the great heraldry that had been contended by British monarchs – and their puppet Parliamentary accomplices - throughout all of the wars that had occurred before this time, the 'Opium Wars' – as they are now named - were the first blatant example of 'nation state' involvement in widespread criminality. A secondary surge of conflict occurred in the year 1856 AD. Although the first conflict was conducted indirectly by proxy, with the use of 'British East India Company' mercenaries, the associated support – comprising Royal Naval gun ships, crewed with combatives – was centrally instigated from London. Likewise, during the second conflict, much more directly. Thus was established, an enormous trading dominion, eventually augmented substantially by French, Prussian and American infiltrations into the Chinese sphere, extending far to the north of Hong Kong, up the Yangtze River to Shanghai, and southwards from Hong Kong through Malaya 'to-be' to Singapore. All of the lands and the populaces of which, provided for new styled produce – such as rubber – to be cultivated and shipped – incredibly cheaply – to Europe and beyond. Most of which kept arriving in Britain in particular, through numerous decades, until the Japanese invaded China, Malaya and Singapore.

The tactic of using incumbents to control their own, is a strategy that has been employed by the British military, for a long time. As a 'Boy Entrant' in the Royal Air Force from the year 1962 AD, I was initially billeted with thirty or so others in a single – very long - wooden hut, which was connected to a network of similar huts, incorporating washrooms and toilets. All of the toilet doors were chopped off from waist level down to deny toilet users of privacy, due to a number of suicide attempts preceding my days there. My entry was the 47th at RAF St Athan, firstly inducted – like all other entries - into an ITS(Initial Training Squadron), separated from other entries for the sake of our safety, for the first three months. Then, duly adapted to the rigours of the place, we were placed with all of the entries that preceded us, of which there were seven, with the 39th entry being senior. It was not wise to be unpopular in this environment. In fact, at worst, it was downright dangerous. At best, it was infuriating. Conformity attacks had to be endured on two fronts, from the adult establishment, supported with QRs(Queens Regulations), and from entries more senior, who imposed covert terror by violent means, often. Entries more senior offloaded their official liabilities – such as boot polishing, toilet cleaning, web polishing – onto junior entry members, requiring standards far beyond normal comprehension. To say, that duly polished boots could be used as mirrors, is not an under statement. With gang styled intimidation prevailing, individuals were forced to think on their feet, in response to rapid changes in moods – and of whole atmospheres – at times. Reprisals for non-conformity – or for lacklustre responses – took the form, most often, of having your personal bed-space wrecked, perhaps with personal injury sustained in the process. Inter-peer bullying was rife. In those days, it was not unusual to be woken in the middle of the night with your bed on top of you, dripping acid water. On a whim, the senior's bravado and belligerence was expended by their night raids on juniors, tipping occupied beds over, shooting lead-acid fire extinguishers on the result. When the adults rampaged to determine the culprits, nobody, but nobody squealed.

Getting back to incumbents, each billet housed a 'Leading Boy' – who could also be a Corporal, Sergeant or Flight Sergeant boy – in a separate room at the end of each billet, who were supposed to keep order – and who were depended on, to squeal – about detrimental events that occurred during the adult's absence. Where official infringements to QRs occurred, these incumbent NCOs(non commissioned officers) were generally effective. Conversely, they were completely ineffective as anti-intimidation police, due to the bonded power of entry rivalry, which ironically, was promoted within official bounds by the adults that 'thought' that they controlled us all. By contrast, their punishments – which extended through greater amounts of time, and which were much more arduous – were preferable to the 'rival entry' order of things. Typically, to compound all of the informal difficulties that persisted, it was possible to be charged for a misdemeanour – such as 'walking across grass' – to receive three days fatigues – scrubbing floors for two hours a day – and end up with thirty consecutive days of the same, by failing a personal inspection; imposed twice a day during fatigues. A slight smudge on a webbing belt, or a small smear on the glass-like surface of a boot toe, was sufficient to fail such inspections. On viewing the plight of Indian incumbent troops, I think of all this, somewhat appreciating – I think – what they went through at the time. Yes, using incumbents is always a risky affair. In my world at St Athan, a number of 'leading' boy NCOs turned out to be homosexuals, causing a massive uproar then. They were gone in a flash, being totally detrimental to the aims and the objectives of the adult establishment. Yet most of all, I remember in particular, one of my colleagues that rose to the dizzy heights of 'Warrant Office' boy, who was sometimes reduced to a nervous wreck, due to his mixed set of responsibilities, and loyalties. I never desired his status.

Section Twenty Eight:
Insane Adventurism

Duly, in the context of the 'whole world', without any sort of pre-determination, by the year 1839 AD, Britain was developing an empire, enforced with the presence of military forces here, there and more or less everywhere, except the 'Americas'. To say that the 'British East India Company' was getting a bit above itself by then, is retrospectively valid. By then – quite newly – queen Victoria was in close cahoots with the prevailing British Prime Minister – Whig Lord Melbourne – who responded positively to Victoria's invitation to take up residence in Windsor Castle, supposedly to teach her the ways of British politics, five days a week, for five hours each day. Rumours were abound then, that Melbourne might become the secondary heir to the thrown by marrying Victoria, but – ironically, if not astonishingly – all dissipated due to a political scandal about Melbourne being involved in sexual spanking sessions at the bed chambers of certain female undesirables. To which, Melbourne offered his resignation. This was not actually invoked due to Sir Robert Peel refusing to form an alternative government, and then, Melbourne just carried on, remaining in Parliament as the Prime Minister, and in Windsor castle, as Victoria's principal tutor. In due course, he even managed to establish numerous positions of patronage in Windsor, for his relatives. I know that you are saying now: "I thought all of this sort of thing was not evident before the days of John Profumo and Christine Keiler?" Yet with the enormous 'British eastern-world' successes of that time, came a proportionate disaster, substantially contributing to the obliteration of the 'British East India Company', strangely in the very same year of the first of the 'Opium Wars', and the Lord Melbourne scandal. By this year, the 'British East India Company' had moved 4,500 mercenary troops from Pakistan 'to-be' through the Khyber pass into Afghanistan as far as Karbul, to establish and to occupy the fort there. As a means of improving morale, trooper wives were permitted to join them, along with all sorts of civilian support personnel, totalling 12,000 non-military people in all. With a number of life-threatening incidents occurring successively, and with strong opposing armies gathering around Karbul, the decision to withdraw was taken, back through the Khyber pass. According to involved witnesses then, the reasons for the initial incursion were vague; something to do with fears about Russian forces taking control of the area, for what reasons nobody knew.

Later in 1843, the army chaplain G.R. Gleig – thought then, to be the sole survivor of this withdrawal attempt, wrote:

"a war begun for no wise purpose, carried on with a strange mixture of rashness and timidity, brought to a close after suffering and disaster, without much glory attached either to the government which directed, or the great body of troops which waged it. Not one benefit, political or military, was acquired with this war. Our eventual evacuation of the country resembled the retreat of an army defeated".

Looking at the bigger picture, all of these events preceded yet another 'Holy Roman Empire' campaign that started on a 'religious righteousness' footing, but which eventually evolved into complicated national territorial exasperations; that of the Crimean War, commencing in the year 1853 AD. British concerns about Nicholas 1st of Russia – a renowned militarist – encroaching on Pakistan 'to-be' and Afghanistan, were apparent just ten years or so before this war started. Even with it finished, they persisted enough – as late as the year 1878 AD – to justify in part anyway, a second – officially sanctioned - military invasion into Afghanistan, lasting just under three years, somewhat catastrophically again. After achieving nominal gains the beleaguered 'red coated' troops, scurried out as quick as they could, just to re-reach safety and salvation.

The only other actual survivor of the initial force, totalling 16,500 people, John Masters – later becoming a Captain in the 4th Foot during the second campaign, recorded in his autobiography: "that Afghan women in the North-West Frontier Province of British India during the Second Anglo-Afghan War would castrate non-Muslim soldiers who were captured, like British and Sikhs. They also used an execution method involving urine; Pathan women urinated into prisoner's mouths. Captured British soldiers were spread out and fastened with restraints to the ground, then a stick, or a piece of wood was used to keep their mouth open to prevent swallowing. Pathan women then squatted and urinated directly into the mouth of the man until he drowned in the urine, taking turns one at a time".

Section Twenty Nine:
British Industrial Hell

On the home front, industrialism proliferated long before the coronation of queen Victoria in the year 1837 AD. In fact, by this time the pig iron foundries in and around Derbyshire were swamped with the demand for materials to be re-processed into 'cast' and 'wrought' iron, for steam engine manufacturing, both static types for factory power, and locomotive types for transport. Particularly, 'wrought iron' manufacturing permutations were infinite – newly massive in scale – for ships(iron clad), bridges, railway networks, canal lock gates and anything else – everywhere – requiring structural robustness. Consequently, the architecture and the whole of the infrastructure in Britain changed radically, within just a few decades, with multitudes of people concentrations in new towns and new factories churning out produce and products – unlike anything of old – for the rest of the world to consume. All distributed nationally and internationally with new railways and with an enormously expanded merchant fleet, supported very substantially by a strong – ruling the waves – Royal Navy. Yet, all of the minions – the paupers and the serfs of old, newly enslaved in factories – not only remained either perpetually exhausted or destitute, but more exhausted and more destitute than their ancestors had been before them. When they were unable to cope – particularly when they fell into ill-health – they endured the 'Poor House' regime. When they fell into debt, they were imprisoned, to work tread-mill contraptions regimentally. When they reached old age, they died, deprived of the privilege of dignified retirement, due to the early expenditure of their physical capabilities. In the meantime, those that owned the means of production, could languish decadently, in the midst of their new-found 'Elderodoes', furnished from a new dirty phenomenon; 'profit'. Also, from profit's subsequent derivative; 'rent'. With a good kick-start into the new wealth creation game, it wasn't even necessary to be remotely involved with it all. The new phenomenon of commercial companies with related 'commercial shares', had arrived, and with it, also arrived 'speculation'. Payment for investment, without actually doing anything.

Yet for a few – who had often been bestowed with some sort of economic propulsion – the order of the 'Knights of the Garter' became penetratable. Britain was soon newly composed, not only of 'the land barons of old', along with all of its destitute minions, but also with newly born – inaptly described – 'entrepreneurs', who, with minor exceptions, had gained phenomenally from international slavery in one way or another, and/or from the newly refined composite of wage labour styled slavery, on the home front. With the Duke of Wellilngton's hatred – the Parliamentary Reforms Act of the year 1832 AD – they wheedled their way with the support of a 'property owning electorate' into Parliament as members, with new powers to influence national political and national economic policies, just like the existing landed gentry. The very same landed gentry that evolved from the original 'barons of old'. With subsequent elevation from 'The House of Commons' to 'The House of Lords' – which occurred naturally with the prevalence of patronage and nepotism – they were often elevated further, to the Queen's Council, truly to become 'Knights of the Garter'. In short, the economic structure of Britain between the years 1750 - or so – and the year 1830 AD had altered radically and phenomenally, but the political control domain remained medieval. William 4th still vied for political power, and Parliament remained – in the main – a monarchical puppet. With the 'Corn Laws' maintained to prohibit the importation of cheaper corn – after the end of the Napoleonic wars between the years 1815-1846 AD – the landed gentry was subsidised, while all of the minions – working in the factories – were forbidden to collaborate, to raise their wages, from the year 1799 AD until the middle of the eighteenth century, during the period that the 'Combination Acts' were enforced. Additionally, from the year 1799 AD many British minions found themselves being shipped to Australian penal colonies, just for committing misdemeanours. In this way, many of the rebels that contributed to the 'grapevines' of the day – invariably disrespectful of the 'establishment' – were extracted, like solitary rotten apples, from a fresh harvest.

By the precedent set in the legal case of 'The Tolpuddle Martyrs', union styled labour collaboration was categorised as a criminal felony, automatically dealt with by means of deportation to Australia, duly instigated in this case. In fact, not a strategy that helped the British economy much at the time. Industrial machinery patent registrations – for new factory machine inventions – diminished considerably. Incentives to replace workers with machines had been removed by the acts. As it turned out – with all of the Napoleonic issues to deal with – the government that ruled at the turn of the eighteenth/nineteenth centuries needed to keep all of the workers in the factories anyway. It had indulged itself in expensive wars with the French, which required expensive war ships, expensive weapons and the expansion of naval/army manpower. For the first time – under the chronic auspices of William Pitt(the younger), tax on employee income was introduced. This was repealed and then re-introduced on numerous occasions, but it remained – and of course it grew – from the year 1834 AD onwards. In the context of all of this, William 4th – and queen Victoria that followed him – had it all ways. They – or should I say, Victoria and Albert(of the house of Saxe Coburg and Gotha) – retained political influence, they waged the wars they wanted to wage, and they got all of the minions – mostly the new factory underlings – to pay for it all.

By the year 1837 AD Charles Dickens, with the publication of his enigmatic story: 'Oliver', was well on the way to telling the world about the skulduggery life of many underlings, in the Britain of his day. Initially, all for audiences that were literate enough to read it, which did not amount to a noticeable portion of the population. Then, those born lowly – most – wishing to better themselves, definitely had the odds stacked against them. Life was all about factory work, mine work, foundry work, day-to-day, and about sleep to recover for the next day, day in, day out, with few comforts. In the cramped urban environments, 'Gin Palaces' appeared everywhere in response to new insatiable demands for temporary relief from the prevailing arduousness. All were laboriously decorated with ground glass embellishments, with fancy mirrors, poised to nicely reflect – to exaggerate with gas light – new warmth and new pleasantness in the midst of dark, dingy streets. In London – the biggest city in the world, then – night life for working types most often consisted of a 'quick flash of lightning' in a gin palace, followed with a raucous evening in a public drinking saloons, that had performance stages, later developed into music halls like 'The Old Mo' in Drury Lane. By the 1850s, the predecessors of Marie Lloyd and Little Tich sang 'community involved' slogan songs, with frequent satirical enhancements. All of which established a new privileged way of spending valuable time in the midst of the prevailing industrial turmoil. The new phenomenon of 'recreation' had arrived, although most were deprived of it, at least until trips to Blackpool and Brighton were born, much later and much after Marie Lloyd enjoyed prominence.

Again, my own experiences link – I think – to the 'British Empire' and to the old music hall atmospheres. Just eighteen, there I was, humming along in a lovely Bristol Britannia for thirty hours, with stops at El-Adem-Libya, Aden-Yemen, Ghan-Maldives, on the way to Changi-Singapore. I had travelled within an elite society, still treading along the old 'British Empire' road, and still making the most of the legacy that it had left. I was part of a detachment of No 55 squadron, RAF to support Victor bomber placements at Tengai, Singapore, as part of the force that opposed President Sukarno of Indonesia in the years 1964-5, in the face of communist ascendancy in the east of the world then. The Vietnam war was raging, not too far away. Previously, I had been enticed to join the RAF as a member of the Air Cadets in Preston, Lancashire. I accompanied my cadet squadron to RAF Jurby on the Isle of Mann for a week during the summer of the year 1960 AD. There I flew aerobatics as a passenger for the first time, and, I experienced a profound roll model, who left a distinct mark on my desires and my ambitions. He was a short – very short – weedly looking soldier of the RAF Regiment, who I first sighted at the Jurby firing range. Stood firmly with legs forward and back, he held a Le Enfield .303 calibre rifle with perfect precision, placing five of its rounds smack into the centre of one of the bulls-eye styled target templates. Have you ever heard a Le Enfield .303? If the butt is not rammed deeply into the shoulder socket of the user, it is an arm fracture contraption. It kicks harder than an adult mule, and it shoots enormous lead lumps for a mile and more, with accuracy up to one thousand yards.

On the completion of this miraculous shooting fete, he responded to the exasperations of my group, by standing – with legs spread – at ease, with his rifle butted to the ground, glorious and satisfied. You see, I stood looking at him for a long time – it seemed then – indeed, unable to detect any sort of blemish on his uniform or his person. He stood there with white spats at his ankles, with razor creases in his trousers, with a tie uniformly tied. All was perfect. Greatly then, I admired his appearance, and moreso, I admired his shooting abilities, and even moreso, when I first attempted to handle a Le Enfield .303 calibre rifle, which I could hardly stop waving around, with all of its weight and all of its devastating power. Nobody, but nobody, was trigger happy with that weapon. When I joined the RAF, I also joined the breed that had left the 'British Empire' legacy in Singapore, and I had joined in time – as it turned out – to experience this legacy. The locals around 'The Raffles Club' – adjacent to the Raffles Hotel – in Singapore, had devised ways to acquire money from British servicemen, long before I arrived. Taking a ride on a rickshaw with some of my pals, the puller invited us: "You want jigajig Jonny, five dollar, ten dollar, twenty dollar?" From a group of four, two of us ventured into China-town with the puller, to be presented to a row of 'cheongsam' dressed tiny women. Immediately, we realised that you take your pick and you make your choice. Could you expect a boy of eighteen to resist?

RAF Tengai was a raucus den in the evenings then. The lads used to pile out – totally stuporfied – out of the Malcolm Club, through the front gate to purchase double egg banjos, at stalls nearby. Taxis – old Mercedes types – standing adjacent to these stalls were used for trips to China-Town, but occasionally – depending on the prevalence of devilment – they were also used to tow the stalls down the causeway road, without the drivers realising. Particularly with the poor old 'Banjo' cookers in hot pursuit, screaming with furious annoyance. This is how the 'drunken gang' got their laughs in those days. Well, one of the ways, anyway. Other methods often mimicked the old Victorian 'music hall' scenario in the NAAFI club. There the drunks – of which I was one at times – used to stand around somebody absolutely 'blind-out-of-his-mind', naked and elevated on a table, slinging Tiger beer all over him as he sang: "Alluetta, shonty Alluetta, how I love your shonty nose, shonty nose, OOOOh, Alluetta, Alluetta". This was a sort of ritual that progressed through all of the usual naughty nuances, to a ridiculous climax. All of the legacy of the 'British Empire'. Yet also, this was a bigoted legacy. The locals were subservients, to be used and sometimes to be abused. They were the 'wogs' and we were the elite. That was the way of it in the British forces, then, just prior to the 'British Empire's' cessation.

At the birth of the nineteenth century, industrialisation in Britain was all about, a chaotic malignancy exasperating all around, in the midst of unprecedented adaptation. In fact, all was an industrial monster, spurting pollution, crowding hopeful people into confined – dangerous – spaces, replacing antique quaintness with bustling vibrance, without much consideration for the eventual outcome of it all. Yet, where 'people' concentrations proved beneficial to factory operations, such concentrations endangered human health, besides obliterating all and sundry of the natural world within the bounds of new towns and cities. Excepting the other slave types of the age; horses. All of the minions gadding about in traps, in coaches, in buses, and in horse drawn buses travelling on wrought iron rails; trams. Mixed up within it all, terraced slums of the new red brick age, with all of the occupants burning the black rock energy source of heat – coal – at the 'downwind' end of new urban 'squalor' dominions, so as not to pollute the elite living upwind. At the start of it all – and still by the year 1800 AD – iron foundries were – in comparison to this age – miniscule and numerous, belching coal and coke smoke into everyone's breathing space, day and night, relentlessly. Can you imagine the stench and the filth? Particularly, can you imagine whatever became of all of the horse manure in the urban streets, and for that matter, all of the human excrement about all of the public vicinities and about all of the tightly packed terraced dwellings of the working underlings? Nothing was organised; nothing was planned. Quite contrastingly, comparative French towns and cities of that era were managed with sensible respect for their incumbent populations, because important infrastructures for public health were created during Napoleon Bonaparte's reign. By the year 1810 AD, Paris benefited substantially from over three hundred kilometres of sewers, with the river

Seine sluiced extensively. Such was Napoleon's legacy.

By the year 1856 AD, extending from the reign of William 4th to queen Victoria – London and many other British cities – were throttled, with impractical living amenities – with all of the horses shitting about the streets everywhere – and with successive public health crisis's, principally due to drinking water being contaminated with sewage. In the year 1831-32 AD, 7,000 Londoners perished due to Cholera, and then it just got worse, by far. Out of the initial 30,000 infected by 'King Cholera' in London during the year 1849 AD, 15,000 perished. The true facts of the time are hereby quoted:

"New epidemics were stalking the cities - cholera and typhoid were carried by polluted water, typhus was spread by lice, and 'summer diarrhoea' was caused by swarms of flies feeding on horse manure and human waste. The problem was easy to identify and difficult to solve. Too little was invested in the urban environment, in sewers, street paving and cleansing, and in pure water and decent housing."

The census of 1851 recorded half of the population of Britain as living in towns - the first society in human history to do so. To quote further:

"A comparison between a desperately unhealthy large town and a small market town shows the costs of migrating in search of work and prosperity. In 1851, a boy born in inner Liverpool had a life expectancy of only 26 years, compared with a boy born in the small market town of Okehampton, who could expect to live to 57."

In the end, it took the phenomenon of 'The Great Stink', occurring in the year 1858 AD, to mobilise the British Parliament. By this juncture, the health situation in London – and elsewhere – had deteriorated about as far as it could, into a continuously occurring national crisis. At least by then, the establishment had got the message. In a hurry somewhat, substantial improvements were implemented, progressively and continuously up to the year 1865 AD. Proportionately, public health improved.

Section Thirty:
The Crimean War

Amidst it all though, the eternal 'Holy Roman Empire' phenomenon raised its snake styled head again. Where Tsar Alexander 1st of Russia had been an instigator of the resurgence of the 'Holy Roman Empire' by being a co-founder of the 'Holy Alliance' in the year 1815 AD, Tsar Nicholas 1st – his successor – surged troops into Turkey to invoke the creeds of the 'Holy Alliance', to protect the interests of orthodox Christians, facing threat. Somewhat coincidentally, just one year before, Napoleon Bonaparte's nephew – initially legitimately elected as France's president – staged a coupe-de-tat to become Napoleon 3rd, the dictator of France. Full of belligerence, especially against all of the probable exponents of 'The Holy Roman Empire', he viewed Tsar Nicholas 1st of Russia to be such a person. Re-living his uncle's legacy somewhat, he was keen to ally France to the prevailing Ottoman regime when it declared war on Russia in the year 1853 AD. With queen Victoria thirteen years into her marriage with 'Albert' and with one of the Duke of Wellington's previous disciples sitting as the Prime Minister of Britain – 'The Earl of Aberdeen', an archdeacon of

'The Old School Tie Brigade', metaphorically speaking – the Royal Navy was able to grasp opportunities to get in amongst the commotion in the Baltic sea. Just imagine the admirals jumping about with excitement about the prospects of a fight, with Victoria and Albert protesting about Russian expansionism, and 'The Earl of Aberdeen' remonstrating with both parties, to be seen as a true British patriot. 'The Earl of Aberdeen' was a busy man. At that juncture, he was only just concluding a second war in Burma.

At that time, numerous anomalies within the British political constitution existed, some of which – to this day – have persisted. Where the Parliamentary reform act of the year 1832 AD provided for the election of 'people representatives' to the House of Commons in order to provide due representation, prevailing governments were composed from both the 'Commons' and the 'Lords', of which, members of the latter were not placed democratically. Membership to the 'House of Lords' was – and still is – decided by inheritance, or by Prime Minister appointment(with the monarch's sanction). Thus, when the Lord of Aberdeen died, his son took his place in the House of Lords. In other words, with the presence of patronising politicians of the 'William Pitt'(the younger, elevated by his father) kind, when   cabinet members wished to create influence and power for a member of their 'brigade' or for a member of one of their 'networks' – most often members of the landed gentry who were hereditary lords - they simply appointed them as ministers; as secretaries of state. The fact that these people did not truly represent anyone – having not been elected – didn't seem to matter. Realise that this strategy – which really amounts to the corruption of democracy – has been adopted frequently and continuously to this day, particularly utilised in recent years by Margaret Thatcher, Anthony Blaire and David Cameron. Taking things to the extreme, with 'Lords' being pseudo legitimately placed into British government cabinets, crony Prime Ministers – and higher level cabinet ministers – can easily place anyone in government. The chosen person is simply 'appointed' to the House of Lords – as a 'Life Peer' – and then plucked from there, into the cabinet, with Secretary of State status, and power, which to say the least, is always formidable. What is to be realised further, is that this situation is greatly extenuated with junior ministers recommending favoured members of their 'brigade' for life peerage status. By this expedient, people like Lord Sainsbury, Lord Nuffield and particularly, Lord Beaverbrook exercised substantial political power. Within British history, the list of such examples persists, ad-infinitum.

Here, to emphasise the immensity of this persistent problem, details within www.wikipeadia about George-Hamilton Gordon – 4th Earl of Aberdeen, are shown below:

Born in Edinburgh on 28 January 1784, he was the eldest son of George Gordon, Lord Haddo, son of George Gordon, 3rd Earl of Aberdeen. His mother was Charlotte, youngest daughter of William Baird of Newbyth. He lost his father in 1791 and his mother in 1795 and was brought up by Henry Dundas, 1st Viscount Melville and William Pitt the Younger. He was educated at Harrow, and St John's College, Cambridge, where he graduated with a Master of Arts in 1804. Before this, however, he had become Earl of Aberdeen on his grandfather's death in 1801, and had traveled all over Europe. On his return to England, he founded the Athenian Society. In 1805, he married Lady Catherine Elizabeth, daughter of John Hamilton, 1st Marquess of Abercorn.

26 January 1828 – 2 June 1828
    Chancellor of the Duchy of Lancaster
20 December 1834 – 8 April 1835
    Secretary of State for War and the Colonies
2 June 1828 – 22 November 1830
    Secretary of State for Foreign Affairs
2 September 1841 – 6 July 1846
    Secretary of State for Foreign Affairs
19 December 1852 – 30 January 1855   Prime Minister

Made a member of the Privy Council In July 1815, this man never held a Parliamentary seat, and therefore never represented anybody other than his Tory patrons in Parliament. Ominously elevated to a position of prominence and prestige by Arthur Wellesley(the Duke of Wellington) in January 1828, without appropriate experience, without suitable knowledge, and with – what proved to be – inadequate abilities. Glory be to the 'Old School Tie Brigade'. What is not altogether appreciated, is that this scenario within all of the echelons of the establishment of contemporary Britain – having never been eradicated – is rife, to this day.

Breaking News:

All of the contentions of the above are duly confirmed on this day: 10th February 2015. Lord Stuart Green, a director of the HSBC bank was recently placed as the Secretary of State for Trade and Commerce by David Cameron, the Prime Minister, without being duly elected. Appointed as a Tory life peer - and thus granted political powers in the House of Lords - by Cameron, he was then immediately elevated to 'Trade & Commerce Minister'. Thus 'The Old Boy Network' prevails. Worse though, Green overseered HSBC when its Geneva, Switzerland branch assisted - actually aided - British subjects of the crown, to 'evade' income tax payment. To date - due to information and data supplied by an HSBC employee whistleblower five years ago - billions of pounds are owed. In the meantime - contrary to numerous political assertions about catching tax cheats - during the same period, only one arrest has been invoked for tax non-payment.

End of Breaking News

Within the British Civil Service – an enormous bureaucratic regime of traditional disproportionate size, consuming vast amounts of valuable resources – where the pretence is continuously professed that recruitment and promotion procedures are 'objective', they are anything but. This declaration is made on the basis of my own experience of employment as a 'Civil Servant' for more than seven years, recently. Commonly, management extracts its favourites from the workplace to provide them with undue time – and resources - for unofficial - corrupt - 'grooming'. These favourites invariably end up in prestigious positions without appropriate knowledge and/or experience, to exist as staunch anti-merit – and anti-equity – exponents, hindering – rather than assisting – those below them. Particularly those striving for improvement. Invariably, they hate 'change'. Conversely, they love tradition because this has given them preference. In short – particularly within most government controlled spheres, including local government – all of the major echelons of control in Britain have ended up rotten, frequently invoking 'closed-door' policies to conceal and/or to disguise the proliferation of all of the corruption. Corruption that has been rife of old, which is still rife. Just the mention of 'Karen Shoesmith', the continuous 'Hillsborough enquiry', Fiona Wolfe, the enquiry involving the sexual abuse of minors within state institutions – of which Lord Leon Britton is detrimentally associated – and most conspicuously the initial appointment of Lady Slotch as the abuse enquiry chair-person, not to mention all of the aberrations of the BBC, with its serious 'Old Boy Network' pay-offs, and with the deplorable ascendancy of Jimmy Saville through all of the years since the 'Clunk-Click' days.

Faced with enormous difficulties at the port of Sevastapol, and faced with the extremely difficult task of transferring war ships from northern Russia – in the Arctic circle – to Russia's southern coast at Sevastopol in the Baltic sea, Nicholas 1st ceded to the British/French/Ottoman alliance, with the Royal Navy dominating the Baltic. Where nearly all wars that preceded this 'Crimean War' were fought with some sort of involvement of religious dynasties, the order – and the motivations – of the world had truly changed. This was the last, largely due to the defeat of a sovereign of 'The Holy Roman Empire'; Nicholas 1st, successor to Alexander 1st, the principal founder of the 'Holy Alliance'. Yet the Hapsburgs and the Papacy lived on, albeit, somewhat quietly. In the meantime, the Royal Navy had gained opportunities to test new styled weapons, in particular, new 'exploding gunnery shells', fired from its battleships onto the Crimean coastline. This was a new war precedent, which in time would pave the way for a completely new strategy of war; that of ballistic devastation, to quell opposition on sea shores, as a prelude to sea-born invasion. A widely adopted strategy during later – more devastating – years. In this context, the Crimean War was a military testing scenario.

Section Thirty One:
Evolving Protestants

While Charles Dickens – by the end of the first quarter of the nineteenth century – became prolific in his quest to tell all about the appalling idiosyncrasies of the industrial revolution, the religious order of the society that it produced became much more sophisticated. Simply of old, all of the regents and the Papacy had colluded to control all of the minions, throughout all of the lands of Europe, and south America. Then Martin Luther, and successively, John Calvin had founded – in the midst of an awful lot of contentious conflict – a cleaner, simpler form of Christianity, previously pioneered really, by the Moravians. All in opposition to the Papacy of Rome, which could not somehow – through all of the wars and all of the contentions of the sixteenth and the seventeenth centuries – manage to dispense with its inherent 'corruption' garb, even with all of the splendour of the renaissance in the northern regions of Italy 'to-be'. In Britain, in the western Germanies and in the Nederland, as the nineteenth century launched itself into the new found inequity of Laizze Faire, in boost mode, Protestants had already divided into Puritans and Separatists. More prominent in the Nederland, freedom loving Separatists contrasted with the Puritans of Britain and the Germanies, more and more through the seventeenth century. In Britain and in the western Germanies, religion became more about discipline, order and restraint, coupled with purposefulness. Characteristically, in newly developing industrial Britain, Puritan-

Anglican Protestantism fragmented further with the launch of John Wesley's 'Free Church of England' in the year 1844 AD. Preaching strategies – of the kind previously undertaken by George Whitefield – outside of churches, expanded ad-hoc congregations all about England and throughout north America, as the new religious movement of 'Methodism'. In conjunction, the extremely disciplined – and somewhat more retracted - order of 'Quakers' evolved, with increasing strength. Through these times, the Anglican church, sustained its first serious setback.

Thus, with the evolvement of Methodism, common 'grapevines' reached new dimensions, especially because all of the minions that were restrained for six days a week in the factories, in the mines, and everywhere else in Victoria's working Britain, were able – within the informal Methodist preaching framework – to congregate in large combined numbers on Sundays. When the weather was preferable, all dressed in their best clothes to enjoy all of the gossip after religious services, often extending their hard earned leisure in the midst of much needed 'recreation' throughout the remainder of the day. In this context, many 'godly' employers shaped the order of their factories, their mills, their enterprises etc in accordance with their religious credence, the most successful of which were 'Quakers', producing Fry's Chocolate, Cadbury's Chocolate, pig iron for Abraham Derby, Roundtree confectionary, Clarke's shoes and money management services within Barclay's and Lloyd's banks, just to mention a few. In conjunction with the accelerated growth of British industries – many of which were inter-dependent and intertwined – a renewed road network evolved to move people around, more efficiently and more rapidly than ever before. All made possible by the likes of Thomas Telford from the year 1810 AD. His efforts produced the St Katherine's docks in London, the great Menai Straights road bridge, over 1,000 miles of new roads and 1,200 bridges. In the meantime, commencing with a pioneering effort with his father to tunnel underneath the Thames river in central London, Isumbard Kingdom Brunel – who died at the young age of 52 years – expended enormous amounts of energy – and enthusiasm – in the continuation of Thomas Telford's endeavours, successfully superceding him by designing and constructing a superior bridge than that initially designed by Telford, over the Avon Gorge at Bristol. As magnificent as the Clifton Suspension Bridge is to this day, on its completion it melted into insignificance with Brunel's subsequent achievements, which include the creation of Temple Meads railway station in Bristol, over 1,000 miles of railway track – with all of the associated bridges and tunnels, of which some are glorious efforts – and three iron clad steam powered ships, which in turn expanded British influence throughout the world. Significantly, the largest of Brunel's steam ships – the Great Eastern, which was the largest in the world on its launch – laid the first telegraph cable across the Atlantic ocean. The third of his steam ships – The SS Great Britain, truly a symbol of Britain's profound industrial legacy - as it stands in a Bristol dry dock, is revered to this day by tourist from all over the world.

Thus, by the time that queen Victoria ascended to the throne, the British economy was rip-roaring along at a breathtaking pace, with proportionate scale expansions and with relentless technological innovations, all of which reverberated well beyond the shores of the motherland, particularly in the direction of the Indian sub-continent, by then colonially and agriculturally usurped by the British East India Company, for the supply of massive quantities of raw materials. Cotton in particular, but also tea. All shipped rapidly and efficiently by a substantial British maritime fleet, but moreso eventually, by new regional railway infrastructures, established - with an abundance of cheap 'navvy' labour - with astonishing rapidity. Of course, all was supported and protected by a colonial army of the East India Company, comprising civilian administrators/managers and military mercenaries. Interestingly, British religious missionaries - of which there were many then – experienced trouble when they ventured inner India, due to strong 'Hindu' and 'Muslim' dominance, adhered to by its incumbents. Amazingly – and somewhat alarmingly – while the Indian minions impulsed themselves along with the British economic way of things, the minions of the African continent – within its interiors especially – remained unaffected. Truly an awful phenomenon for far reaching religious zealots, compulsed to free the world of savagery, to find the salvation of Christ for all and sundry without faith. At the birth of the Victorian age, large parts of the world contrasted to the extreme. Catholicism – under the direction of the Papacy and 'The Holy Roman Empire' – was all about the European land mass, still, particularly in the two Sicilies, in all of the Mediterranean islands and eastwards as far as Ottoman territory, and very ominously throughout the south American continent. Additionally, its derivative Protestantism – with all of its Methodist and Quaker sub-derivatives – had successfully entrenched itself in the western regions of Europe and in virtually all of the north American continent. Yet all of the inner reaches of the African continent remained an enigmatic void.

Section Thirty Two:
Opening The Vast Lands

What of the industrious and the diligent David Livingstone, then? Of working class origins, graduating himself in medicine and religion, did he aspire to religious missionary ambitions first and foremost – as is contended in most conventional history media – or did he just aspire to adventure into the unknown, with just plain decent compulsion? Who really knows? That he was a great exploring pioneer, is now established beyond doubt. By the year 1842 AD he had penetrated farther north of the Cape Colony frontier than any other white man. The first to reach Lake Ngami in the year 1849 AD, he discovered Victoria Falls in the year 1855 AD, and he pushed further east of Lake Tanganyika than had been previously achieved, although he failed to find the source of the Nile in the midst of all of his searches up to the year 1871 AD. By which time, events near to him and on the north American continent catastrophically evolved, not at all to do with religious ideology conflicts of old, but to do with the retention and the acquisition of valuable economic resources. In the wake of the great 'Abolition Movement' in the American north east, cotton cultivation by means of slaves became one of Abraham Lincoln's principal political issues. In the process of state unionisation to form a federalised nation, the strongly 'Protestant' populace of the north east – by far the largest – demanded universal slavery abolition. Contravening somewhat, the wealth and the power interests of those cultivating cotton in the southern regions. In consequence, the American civil war raged initially at the 'Battle of Bull Run' in the year 1861 AD, eventually with the involvement of nearly two and a half million soldiers, until General E. Lee surrendered in the year 1865 AD. Slavery was duly abolished in the new United States of America, but truly the USA at that time, was only united by oppression. The southern states were not – and still, are not – united in heart, particularly because the distinct African heritage of many of the incumbents remained – and still remain – conspicuous. Often contrasting sharply with the 'long-ago' descendents of the old 'Holy Roman Empire', whose grandparents had experienced all of its distinct ramifications.

Characteristically, the technology of those days was spurred by events, none more potent than the events of war. The new exploding artillery shells of Crimean war battleship fame were refined and miniaturised soon afterwards, in time for the US civil war. These in turn enabled Richard J. Gatling to invent the world's first infantry gun that fired new styled 'bullets' in successive automatic sequence, from a ten barrel formation, rotated by means of a hand cranking handle; the Gatling Gun. Suddenly, the attritional number of fatalities on battlefields increased to unprecedented quantities, much more profoundly, even of 'Pizzaro's canons in the Spanish/Portuguese invasions of Cuba and the south Americas. By the year 1865 AD, along with the Gatling Gun, rotary styled printing presses – which had already expanded the growth of printed media in north America – were superceded with 'Web Presses', invented by Richard March Hoe. Passing rolled paper at speeds up to 20mph, printing up to 60,000 copies per hour, 'Web Press' produced newspapers arrived in the United States of America, in the same year as its true birth as a nation. Consequently, all of its minions became substantially assisted, should they wish, to elevate themselves into the realms of literacy, although – with the prevailing absence of state funded – and state supported – education, this quest remained only within the ambitions of self determinants. Importantly though, through the range of all of the activities of the 'Hoe' family in America, with just a short lag of ten years or so, 'Rotary Printing(Robert Hoe') and 'Web Printing(Richard March Hoe') printing revolutions occurred also throughout Europe. By which time, the Papacy's monopoly of literature production had disappeared into the realms of extinction. These events were not 'pinnacle' for the times however.

By the year 1869 AD, the last spike was driven at Promonontory Summit – 1,085 miles – inland from the American east coast, to inaugurate the first East to West, and West to East railway. Then, with the aid of new exploding shelled rifles, the American 'Buffalo' was annihilated, and then, Geronimo led his tribe of 4,000 braves into revolt. Meanwhile, Germany and Italy in Europe did not exist – even yet - as 'whole entity' nations. While Giuseppe Garibaldi recruited men for his army to exterminate the 'Papacy' in Rome, Franz Joseph 1st(Emperor of Austria and King of Hungary) annexed Venicia. Within seven years of these events, queen Victoria would become the Empress of India, firmly establishing official British rule in this nation, held from that juncture, by regiments of soldiers directly controlled by the British government. With the Suez canal 'yet-to-be' the original colony of the Dutch East Indies Company at the southern tip of the African land mass – established by the year 1652 AD – was contested successively, particularly vigorously during the Napoleonic wars. An important shipping recluse for British maritime excursions to India and beyond, of which Napoleon Bonaparte wished to dominate. Yet of old – since queen Elizabeth 1st's reign – Britannia ruled the waves. Substantial

British entrenchment occurred in this vicinity by the year 1806 AD, which through the decades that followed, was consolidated. With queen Victoria's world empire operating in boost mode at the conclusion of the Crimean war, and the Burma wars, and the Opium wars in China – the Zulu kingdom – directly adjacent to Cape Colony, to the north – was inevitably threatened by the British expansionist trend of the day. By the year 1878 AD, Zulu king Cetshwayo and his braves acquired a lot of 'imperial' respect, consequent of their military victory against British imperialist troops at the battle of Isandlwana. Cetshwayo made the British pay a heavy price for the possession of his lands, which he ceded to eventually. All was spurred back in Britain with new styled newspapers – of which half of the population could not read – extolling the magnificence of the heroes of Roark's Drift, without much mention of the Isandlwana catastrophe. The remaining illiterate half of the population – by word of mouth – were then subjected to stupendous remonstrations about the glory and the magnificence of it all. The newspapers of the day – produced cheaply in large quantities, due to new 'Hoe' styled technology – became in reality, a new 'establishment' weapon of the supplementary war – within all of the military wars – of winning the hearts and minds of the incumbent British populace. Not much different really, to the Regent/Papacy conspiracy of old, existing since Charelmagne was crowned.

Section Thirty Three:
Minion Deceptions Abound

You see, such was the ignorance of all of the underling minions of the world. Information contained in typeset print is made up of facts that are always 'true'. Of old, this notion has existed in ignorant minds, because those with authority – the squeaky clean bashers with the Bible in hand – are to be revered as exponents of the truth; the truth of God, which is ultimate. Of old, regents are crowned by such exponents, at Avignon and in Rome by the Pope of the day, or by their archbishop agents, or alternatively by Protestant agents of this kind who are equivalent. Books propagated this theme for centuries, since the invention of letterpress printing technology, and when newspapers arrived – big-time – overall perceptions – or should I say misconceptions – remained. Believe it or disbelieve it, in contemporary Britain, many people faithfully believe what they read in the Sun and the Daily Star 'rif-raf' tabloids. Likewise, when a crank places an official looking sign 'forbidding dogs on the grass', most conform to it without questioning its legality. It is all to do with conditioning, of the kind that has existed through all of the centuries of Regency/Papacy and Regency/Protestancy domination, through all of the generations that have been oppressed into conformity. This is strongly – to this day – a European phenomenon, which really is an abhorrent human aberration. Personally, during my time in the Royal Air Force I used to walk in straight lines across lawns and grassy verges, in total contravention to the 'gospel' rule not to do so. Not just for the hell of it, just to rebel, but to shorten walking distances in my own interest. After all, in accordance with the philosophies of Adam Smith, the pursuit of individual interest amounts to the aggregate interest of all. In this context, double standards are about everywhere. Everywhere in Britain nowadays, there are assertive signs about, telling people what not to do, many of which are not legally enforceable. Also, there are many others, telling people to do, what, by convention, they already know they need to do. Illegitimate power mongers are everywhere, most often dictating in the depths of printed media. All of this is otherwise known as the 'Rupert Murdoch Phenomenon'.

While most – if not all – of the minions in Britain remained uneducated – actually, an indefinable factor in relative terms – by the start of queen Victoria's rule, some had received sufficient tuition to enable them to read in a rudimentary fashion. In the midst of all of the industrial chaos, just a few philanthropists existed with aims to decently employ – in particular – children with supplementary educational provisions. Some of these were ardent socialists at the start, of whom Robert Owen – Managing the New Lanark Mill in Scotland in the year 1816 AD – was typical. By the year 1818 AD, Henry Brougham and James Mill established an infant school in London on the New Lanark model, but nothing else of this nature occurred until 'The Home and Colonial Institution' was founded in 1836 by the Reverend Charles Mayo, to establish infant schools and to train teachers for them. However, this was the thin edge of a wedge, driven into the blighted poor of the day, with insincere religious indoctrination intentions. Typically, within this new 'Darwinian' age, children were widely 'Gospel' indoctrinated, often to extremes. Also often, factory owners and large land owners – so called philanthropic overseers – funded school building projects – for the education of the children of their employees - and invited the Anglican church to manage them. Caring little about what was taught, in this way they were seen to be 'do-gooders'. Largely due to children being subjected to over-frequent religious worshipping sessions – and even to Gospel 'Earth creation' assertions in preference to Darwinism –

an immense amount of animosity evolved with parents. Enough for these issues to be raised in Parliament by the year 1875 AD. At this juncture, with the British population reaching twenty two million or so, the Anglican church controlled about one third of infant child education for the poor. Contrastingly, the wealthy were provisioned well in this regard as early as the mid 1820s. Children – boys more often than girls – entering prestigious private schools like 'Rugby' as infants, were contiguously prepared for eventual university placement, whereas working class underlings rarely progressed further than acquiring reading – and perhaps writing – abilities, before being re-directed into 'on-the-job' vocational training. Yet all children of that age – by convention – were subjected to an enormous amount of religious influence, one way or another. In particular even after the introduction of the 'Elementary Education Act(1893) and the Balfour Act(1902) – which removed the Anglican church's control of education – they were indoctrinated through daily morning worship sessions, and through a multiplicity of religious ceremonies.

Section Thirty Four:
Germany And Italy Evolve

Here is another subsequent plot; with the production of new newspapers commencing in the mid 1870s, the stories of the establishment, told by the establishment, evolved in the throws of a new phenomenon, that of 'mass media'. Never as before, sufficient numbers of newspapers were produced for all of the adults of the population, who increasingly – without having to depend on grapevines – could directly read the contents, which largely counter-argued with the prevailing 'grapevines' of the rebellious. Immensely, the power of the establishment was increased, and proportionately, public conformity intensified. The establishment was queen Victoria, and her close compatriots for most of the time, Lord Melbourne and Benjamin Disraeli of the Tories, who controlled the British means of manufacture/production, and the 'Mass Media', and many of the wars that were raging about the world, but not all. In fact, four or so decades after the battle of Waterloo, battles not concerning Britain were raging successively in Europe, principally to expel Hapsburg troops from the northern regions of Italy 'to-be', commencing in the year 1848 AD. During this year, Giuseppe Garibaldi – with his 'Red Shirts' army - fought the Austrians in the Turin vicinity, around Lombardy and around Piedmont, and then he marauded throughout the Papacy dominions around the two Sicilies. Most notably – unbeknown to him then – he altered the course of European history by successfully banishing Pope Pius 9th from Rome. Truly, he accelerated the extermination of the remnants of the 'Holy Roman Empire' and nullified – if only temporarily – its derivative, the 'Holy Alliance'. Yet Garibaldi's struggle for the unification of the domains of Italy 'to-be' was a long one, due to the expedients of Napoleon 3rd, the belligerent, egotistical presidential leader of France, at the time. Married to yet another catholic zealot, he placed French troops in Rome soon afterwards, to reinstate and to protect the Pope, and he kept them there until Italy was truly born in the year 1870 AD. While paradoxically supporting the cause of Italian unification, he ousted Garibaldi and forced him into exile, duly undoing all of his efforts. Effectively back-tracking the unification process. Just as if he considered that all of the Papacy issues were exclusive in the midst of Italian power politics, soon afterwards, he involved French troops with those of the

Piedmont/Lombardy regent, Victor Emmanuel 2nd, to expel the Hapsburgs of Austria from Emmanuel's regencies. Then, after sustaining significant military losses at the battle of Solferino – with the Austrians backing away – he changed his mind about the worth of all of the effort. Autonomously in peace negotiations at Villafranca in the year 1859 AD, he undid all of Gariboldi's previous efforts, by re-establishing the legitimacy of the thrones of the dukes of Parma, Modena and Tuscany. Within this new – Hapsburg free – framework, Victor Emmanuel 2nd assumed overall sovereignty with the conclusion of territorial adjustments at Nice and Savoy. Both were returned to France, having been forfeited to the Hapsburgs at the conclusion of the wars with Napoleon Bonaparte.

Yet again then, the Papacy in Rome survived. Gariboldi was back to square one. In the meantime, Europe remained in turmoil, buried in a large heap of uncertainty, due to Napoleon 3rd who refused to respect the terms of the 2nd French republic. As the elected president of the nation, he was expected to withdraw from power at the end of his four year term. On refusing in the year 1851 AD, he became a dictator. A bit of an idiot styled one, at that. Like Charles 1st of England with a catholic zealot of a wife, he contrived and he conspired within France to appease all of his Catholics, whilst simultaneously almost, bouncing around the international scene – quite above himself – in the throws of the Crimean war, of which he was a prominent antagonist. Within a short period – in the midst of Napoleon's international belligerence - a most ominous, and one of the most dangerous military conflicts - of which Britain played no part, and to which it had no particular interest – occurred in Europe. Here throughout the 1860s decade, Otto Von Bismarck (1st Chancellor of Prussia, and eventually, all of newly formed Germany) realised the true jeopardy of Prussia, which started the decade as a relatively weak regency, and also, of the affiliates of the loose German confederation, that existed then. The confederation was made up from a multiplicity of self preservative regencies and dominions, none of which were uniquely powerful enough to resist an invasion of a large neighbouring nation, such as France(in particular), Austria or Denmark. A particular problem of that time – and substantially during later times – was the ethnic mix of the people at the periphery of the confederation, bordering neighbouring nations; especially in the north adjacent to Denmark, within Schleswig(Danish speaking) which was unioned with Holstein(German speaking). By the year 1864 AD, Bismarck's anxieties – born of a regency succession in Schleswig – about a Danish invasion, were realised. Where Prussia – in support of the ethnic Germans – had successfully repelled a previous Danish invasion through the years of 1848-52 AD, it was forced to console with the Austrian Hapsburgs, for military support to repeat the process. By the successful exclusion of the Danes again by the year 1865 AD, Schleswig became part of Prussia and Holstein became part of Austria, just temporarily in the year 1866 AD.

This split had been pre-arranged between Bismarck and the Hapsburgs prior to the conflict, but the Austrians reneged on realising the true 'new' extent of Bismarck's military power. When the Hapsburgs attempted to involve the German confederation in matters of rule in Schleswig-Holstein, Bismarck launched a war against them, with the knowledge that Victor Emmanuel 2nd – the monarch of Lombardy and Piedmont, the northern domains of Italy 'to-be' - would launch simultaneous military attacks on Austrian troops, to the south of Austria within Venetia. Easily, Bismarck had previously concluded this arrangement with Victor Emmanuel 2nd, due to long standing contentions over Venetia between Italian nationals 'to-be' and the Hapsburgs. Succinctly then, Bismarck had contrived to divide his enemy's forces at the crucial juncture of confrontation. The consequence of which, was the nullification of Austrian forces, in the north and in the south, forcing the Hapsburgs to cede Schleswig-Holstein to Prussia and Venetia to Victor Emmanuel's nationalists'. At that juncture(1866 AD), Prussia dominated the northern Germanies, with a significant strength increase.

The pre-emptive strike strategy – of the kind adopted by Bismarck – is very understandable by persons that have experienced similar – perhaps a little less magnamonious – situations in their lives. My father, wishing to get on with his own life without me – after extracting me from my extended family in Wales – often dumped me onto his friends. Most often they were crude, rough associates of his with kind hearts. I discovered through these 'dumping' sessions, that the two virtues often match. Quite similar to my father's mother, who was a bit of girl, but with a heart of gold. Anyway, on a number of occasions I found myself co-habiting with a family in Cleethorpes, at the opposite side of England, but strangely, still with a beach to walk on, as I had in Blackpool. Walking along this one day, a tall older boy and his shorter, younger brother encountered me with a lot of bravado and a lot of threats. The elder had some notion about his young brother being tougher than me, and he was duly encouraged to demonstrate this. There I stood, faced with some critical options. Should I let the younger bully me in an attempt to quell the violent threats of his elder? No. This would not work. The elder would just consolidate the confrontation. Should I tackle the elder directly, with the knowledge that the younger would acquiesce as a consequence? The elder was bigger than me. If I failed, then both would extend the assault, as a matter of training for the younger. The elder sat on the sea wall holding a bow and arrow, pontificating to the younger, who stood in front of me, not so sure of himself. Is it instinct, or what? In an instant I calculated the situation correctly. I gave the younger an almighty thump, and ran. On my way, I felt an arrow grazing my leg, but I was surely free due to the elder having to console his brother. Luckily, my father removed me from that place, soon afterwards. People are forced into this sort of thing, at times. Aggression matters are never simple, especially when they are provoked.

Such events were important to the British only in the context of distracted advantage. While wrangles persisted in the Germanies, the whole of the German populace remained locally distracted from the international scene, leaving Britain free to exploit David Livingstone's discoveries in darkest Africa, with some French competition to contend with, but also - without due anticipation - eventual contentions by Leopold 2nd of Belgium. In the meantime, the clever 1st Chancellor of Prussia, Otto Bismarck – who had by the year 1869 AD unified the north and the central areas of Germany 'to-be' – strove for the integration of the loose regencies in the south of the German speaking lands, into the realms of the Prussian king of the day, Wilhelm 1st of Prussia. In the face of the Austrian Hapsburg dynasty, this objective was almost unrealistic, considering that Austrians are also German speaking. With Spanish political upheavals occurring frequently, and with the imminence of a Spanish royal succession, he manoeuvred within European diplomatic circles to place a German speaking Prussian king on the Spanish throne, probably just to incite agitation in the direction of Napoleon 3rd. He made great play of Napoleon's demands: 'Never to attempt to repeat such actions, again' to Wilhelm 1st, duly altering Welhelm's official reply, in a way that provoked Napoleon's retaliation.

In the meantime, the Prussian army had been strengthened and refined to extraordinary levels. With strong catholic ties existing between Napoleon 3rd and the loose southern regencies of the Germanies – Baden Wuttenburg and Bavaria in particular – were ordinarily French allies, but their loyalties were firmly tested when Napoleon 3rd declared war on Prussia, as a result of Bismarck's provocation. Prussia, even though it had become strong, was part of the Germanies, under threat from an alien nation. As accurately predicted by Bismarck, the southern German regencies supplied troops to side with Prussia in its defence. The end result of which, was the defeat of the French army through successive battles – the last of which was the battle of Sedan - the invasion of France as far as Paris, and the rapid abdication of Napoleon 3rd. Importantly also – after France agreed to the payment of reparations and to the Prussian annexation of Alsace and half of Lorraine – the 3rd French republic was formed. Even more importantly, using the heat of the moment in the immediate wake of the French-Prussian war, within the ominous palace of Varseilles, Bismarck founded the new single nation of Germany in the year 1871

AD. All had been a long, long haul. Most ominously, the Hapsburg Austrians were kept out of it all.

By the time that French troops were withdrawn from Rome and its surrounding districts to support France's war with the Germans 'to-be' in the year 1870 AD, Guisseppe Gariboldi – with his Red Shirts army – had recovered from his setbacks in 1859 AD, enough to conquer Sicily and the whole of southern Italy 'to-be', inclusive of Naples. In the meantime, Victor Emmanuel 2nd had become well entrenched in the north, enough to claim himself – rather prematurely - the monarch of united Italy in the year 1860 AD. Belatedly, this became a reality as Gariboldi finalised with a substantial assault on Rome, within the heart of Pope Pius 9th's Holy See in the year 1870 AD, just after the French occupying troops vacated. Garibaldi, a soldier partisan – without political portfolio, of the 'Risorgimento' movement - gave birth to the new nation of Italy, and then magnanimously retracted, leaving Victor Emmanuel 2nd to move court from Turin to Rome to enjoy his prominence. Also however, the twice banished Pope Pius 9th also returned to Rome, to become a 'prisoner' within his Holy See, which was better than exile. All to fall eventually however, in the face of Mossolini. A strange parody indeed. Both Mossolini and Hitler – two of the world's most notorious dictators/war mongers, rising in unison from the youngest of European nations, born within a year of each other.

Section Thirty Five:
Africa Subdued

In the same year as the birth of Germany as a single nation, the British roving journalist Morton Stanley ventured from the east coast of Africa in search of David Livingstone, who by that time, was beginning to lose his health, due to the arduousness of the African environment. A legend existed then, that Livingstone had been saved from absolute peril – by an African marksman - in the mouth of a lion, about to perish. With the lion duly shot, he survived with just a break in his arm. Soon afterwards, Stanley and Livingstone met, with Stanley enquiring famously in the initial instant: "Doctor Livingston I presume?". During later years, in the midst of subsequent searches by Stanley, Livingstone perished of multiple diseases. When his body was exhumed to be returned to Britain, an autopsy revealed that his arm had been graunched and broken. Thus the 'Livingstone' legend was corroborated. The British establishment of that time – and for that matter, the American establishment also – through their 'Old Boy Networks' in newspaper media, made Livingstone a hero – deservedly – and an icon, to be glorified and to be admired by all of the younger generations of their nations. Undoubtedly he fitted snugly into that age. The church glorified him as one of their marvellous missionaries, and the establishment glorified him because he had bravely ventured with risk to life and limb, truly verified with the lion incident. Both of these society factions entrenched themselves, deeper into authority and influence by this means. By the all powerful newspaper media, posthumously, Livingstone was made a national hero, in an age of rising nationalism, newly invigorated in Europe, especially with the evolvement of the new Italian and German states. Such was the new power of the 'new' newspapers. From that time, the establishments of Britain and America – and most others operating within 'democracy' – realised the advantages of keeping newspaper media magnates in their folds.

Stanley's probable desires to be recorded in history as one of Livingstone's counterparts became substance less, with his subsequent involvement with king Leopold 2nd of Belgium. Acting as Leopold's agent, he identified many circumstances, environments and resources in the Congo river basin of mid-Africa that were potentially exploitable to enhance Leopold's wealth. Easily achieved in the event, within the virgin jungle lands, rich with natural minerals, and with an abundant indigenous populace, potentially to be controlled and/or to be enslaved. Here, Leopold utilised existing tribal rivalry to establish an administration that largely ran itself, in a similar fashion to the East India Company's tactics in India, using indigenous troops to control Indians. In Leopold's Congo, Hutu tribesmen worked Tutu slaves to usurp Congo land and Congo minerals. All to fill Leopold's coffers.
With 'Leopold' aristocracy styled class distinction implemented between indigenous tribes, the 'Congo Free State' evolved through the 1880s and the 1890s into a nation of barbary, enough for it eventually to be officially annexed by the Belgian government in the 1908 AD. Simultaneously - in the same year that Stanley and Livingstone met – Cecil Rhodes joined his brother in the Cape Colony to found 'De-Beers Consolidated Mines' by the year 1888 AD, which – within three years of its formation – produced ninety percent of the world's diamonds. Thus, king Leopold 2nd of Belgium and Cecil Rhodes of Britain were the big men of the

day in Africa, at the time when a scramble for all of its resources began in earnest, propagated and promoted most of all by Rhodes. Not content with his new found wealth, he became – within just a few years – a megalomaniac of the glorious British Empire. Gaining political prestige, he duly formed the British South Africa Company, on discovering a closely guarded secret of the Dutch Boer colonies, to his north.

From the days of the original Cape Colony, the Boer people had managed to co-exist as farmers with the indigenous Zulu of the Ndebele kingdom. Also, they co-existed in Bechuanaland, ruled by chief Lobengula. By the time Rhodes arrived on the African scene, they had established the provinces of the 'South African Republic' and the 'Orange Free State' in the regions of Bloemfontein, Johannesburg, and Pretoria. Living austere lifestyles, Boers were not much interested in glory or riches. Yet fate had cast them a serious blow. Trying very hard to conceal it in the initial instant, eventually, word about 'gold' being abundant in their lands, leaked in Rhodes's direction. Consequently, chief Lobengula was soon appeased by Rhodes, with digging concessions duly negotiated, but the Boers were not much interested in wealth, power and Empires, synonymous with Rhodes's approaches to them. Their refusals to co-operate encouraged substantial land encroachments within their territories, by many British – gold mania afflicted – colonialists, all in the midst of the Kimberley gold rush, and numerous others of the kind. Then of course by the year 1889 AD, Rhodes was able to secure a charter for his British South Africa Company from the British government, in pursuit of the Boer's gold, with British troops to protect this new important British interest, and the interests of the British colonialists that were already encroaching Boer land. Through that marvellous Michael Caine/Stanley Baker film 'Zulu', we all know the fate of the Zulu tribes of the day. Likewise, chief Lobengula and his people fell within the deadly – militarily driven - ambitions of Rhodes, even though they had previously provided mining concessions. Inevitably, it was only a matter of time before Rhodes and the president of the South African Republic – Paul Kruger – clashed, not solely due to Rhodes's quest for gold, but also because British troops extended their land occupations further northwards into Bechuanaland, later to be re-named after Rhodes, as Rhodesia.

Within all of his dreams, Rhodes even aspired to the creation of a continuous railway from Cape Colony to Cairo, but a significant turn of events – of his making – diverted the attention of the British military. Soon afterwards in the year 1889 AD, Paul Kruger decided that enough was enough. So started 'The Boer War', taking the British nation – at its most dastardly – into the twentieth century. Realise this, that throughout this war, British newspapers did not refer to the 'South African Republic' by its authentic name, but instead continuously referred to it with the alternative colloquialism: 'Transvaal'. All was within the working framework of the British establishment's 'hoodwinking' tactics, of old, newly propagated within newspapers. Millions of them all about British lands, for all of the newly literate to read, most of whom however, remained uneducated. Greedy Uitlanders – as the Boers named them – were not welcome in the lands of the 'Horn', in the Boer lands. When they were denied political rights by Paul Kruger, the force of the British military was applied. Not particularly well, during the preliminary period however. Nationalist sentiments, whipped up locally by the British High Commissioner: Alfred Milner, were really subordinate in the minds of most mining capitalists. In fact, a lot of the conflict was to do with the eggshell egos of people like Milner and Rhodes, much compounded a year or so after the start of it all with the placement of the 'mad Marhdi suppressor', General H.H. Kitchener. Truly a zealot of the extreme military approach to life, according to his legacy of Boer war fame. The truth of the matter was that the British government of the day, in the face of fierce Boer resistance - much enthused by new belligerent upstarts like the young Winston Churchill – increased troop numbers to suppress Paul Kruger's South African Republic, enough to outnumber Boer fighters by two to one.

Faced with this situation, Kruger compatriots vacated their homes and adopted guerrilla warfare tactics, most effectively. In fact, effectively enough to nullify the conventional tactics initially adopted by Kitchener. Truly the measure of the man was tested. Rather than face humiliation at home, he turned ruthless to the extreme. With the realisation that Boer families were left defenceless in their homes without their men folk, he sent his troops – the so called righteous troops of the queen Victoria – to bully, butcher and imprison them, burning all of their homes to the ground in the process. All were then 'concentrated' in wire fenced camps, deplorably inadequate for the maintenance of basic human health, in terms of food provision, hygiene or medical care. In total, 75,000 direct Boer dependents were imprisoned in this way, along with 20,000 or so black Boer servants. The numbers that died as inmates due to malnutrition and due to disease is not known, but there were many. Ominously, and characteristically – in the midst of all of the British establishment conspiracies of the time – none of this information reached the British public. The contents of the British newspapers of the day, were all about the glories of the relief of the Mafeking siege. According to people like Milner: "All was worth it" he roused, on receiving a congratulatory telegram from queen Victoria". In the midst of the war, Churchill the younger, who was directly active as a war correspondent – but who was actually fighting belligerently with British troops – omitted Kitchener's 'cottage burning' atrocities from his reports. Although he was not directly implicated, these omissions substantiate that he was a co-conspirator of the campaign of silence that followed. His ideas about war reporting included the telling of his glorious story, about how he had escaped, concealed in a railway wagon, after he had been captured. When all was summarised, the Boer war had really been about encroaching on Dutch pioneers, again!

Section Thirty Six:
Steel

The British East India Company was born in this way, and now – without shame – so was the Elderado of the Empire, that of South Africa, as it would become. Unlike the Spanish that invaded Peru however, subsequent British rule imposed no religious doctrines. The Boer war was not in any way a religious war, like all of the ones of old. It was a political war, in the midst of a new capitalist world, which cared nothing about religious convictions. Yet the true exponents of the so called defunct 'Holy Roman Empire', looked on, not at a distance, but through the eyes of the German military attaché on the scene, at the time. For all of its glory, the foundations of the British

Empire at the time of Livingstone and Leopold – in the midst of queen Victoria's rule – were creaking, even at the juncture when Victoria became the Empress of India in the year 1877 AD. Cotton supplies from the southern states of America were somewhat strangled, due to the American civil war. Worse, the advent of the abolition of slavery – which Britain had pioneered – reduced the likelihood of these supplies being rejuvenated. Yet, new plantations had in the meantime been established in India. Regardless, the cotton supply situation into Britain deteriorated seriously, disaffecting traditional British textile outputs, with raw cotton costs rising, and with frequent strikes at Lancashire mills, with workers rebelling against wage reductions. Yet with phenomenal growth rates within the derivative industries of the nation, offsetting monetary/trade compensations were evident. The rapid expansion of the national rail network, with the building of tracks, bridges and viaducts all about the English, Scots and Welsh lands substantially stimulated the production of wrought iron. Docks with cranes, and lots and lots of merchant ships, increased foundry activity even more. Still full of zeal in its economy, British inventiveness, striding forward in great leaps by the year 1856 AD, gave birth to 'steel', with all of its associated ramifications.

The Henry Bessemer steel manufacturing process that appeared from this juncture provided the means of a secondary surge of industrialism, firstly occurring in Britain, but permeating into Europe and the USA within two decades. Since, the world across Russia, Japan, Europe, Britain and a lot of the Americas has churned this material out – often hammer forged – in vast quantities to create and to alter infrastructures, to phenomenal – world changing – proportions. By the 1870s decade,

Sheffield steel products infiltrated European domestic environment, all about. Cooking utensils, cutlery, machinery components of all kinds, all just in time for the advents of the 'internal combustion engine' and 'electricity generation'.

Even with its hands directly placed on substantial diamond and gold resources – as a consequence of Boer subversion – Britain's economic advantages were nullified by the year 1850 AD. The Austro-Prussian and the Franco-Prussian wars spurred steel production in Germany 'to-be' within successive Krupp industrial dynasty control. Germany, newly born in the 1871 AD, entered the world with a massive steel production clout, matching British outputs by the 1880s, but succinctly, only marginally exceeding William Carnegie's industrial empire of steel in Pittsburg, USA. Germany, the strongest of the three at that juncture, piled up the international pressure, towards Africa in a manic scramble to acquire resources, in hot pursuit of Britain, France and Belgium, establishing German East Africa – later to become Tanganika – in the year 1884 AD, and German South West Africa – later to become Namibia – in the same year. Great chunks of African land, some of which in the east, infringed upon the old Portuguese colony of Mozambique. Contrastingly, the USA restrained itself within its national boundaries, propelling its Pittsburg centred steel economy – with tremendous force and with phenomenal impact – into the realms of future world domination. Meanwhile, conditions for workers – well within the midst of widespread industrial slavery – improved in Britain, throughout Europe – even with the prevalence of political upheaval – and in north America. Industrialism provided more material gains for most of the individuals within these nations.

Section Thirty Seven:
British Philanthropy And Charity

Yet, all of the minions of Africa – newly indoctrinated with the zeal of Christian missionaries from all about Europe – remained subservients, mostly slaves to some sort of cause, duly focused on European interests. Additionally, all of the minions of Russia still existed in their traditionally backward agrarian environs, still idolising Tsar Alexander 2nd. Also, similar circumstances prevailed throughout Behemia during these times. Surprisingly though, in the east of the world sprang a new industrial participant: Japan. Of which, after numerous struggles with Russia extending through half a century and more, the world would hear about in a big way. With the words of Charles Dickens resounding about by the mid 1850s and with the delirium and the destitution of the inhabitants of Britain's growing industrial cities, with Cholera, Typhoid and Smallpox abound, quite an undercurrent styled movement existed in the midst of those that possessed a sizeable amount of wealth, to alleviate the suffering of the poor, even from the early years of the nineteenth century. The Labourer's Friend Society was founded by Lord Shaftsbury in England in the year 1830 AD. Created to raise poor standards, this promoted cottage land husbandry, to increase the supply and the quality of the food for land labourers, which evolved eventually into the allotment movement. Increasing in popularity – particularly during the two world wars – allotment land husbandry is to this day, a widely practiced activity. By the year 1850 AD, a number of trusts funded by the wealthy – particularly the Peabody Trust and the Guinness trust – were founded with philanthropic intentions. Earlier, a pioneering charitable organisation was founded by Captain Thomas Coram, who was appalled by the number of abandoned children living on the streets of London. He financed Foundling Hospital in 1741 to look after these unwanted orphans in Lamb's Conduit Fields, Bloomsbury. This was the first such charity in the world, serving as the precedent for incorporated associational charities everywhere. One of which later, named Dr Bernado's Homes grew from virtually nothing to national magnitude, but this organisation has been tainted somewhat by its involvement in the activity of shipping orphans to Canada, New Zealand, South Africa and Australia – mainly during the post WW2 years – to work as virtual slaves for old styled colonialists, within the colonialist ethos that existed at that time.

With 'The Society of Friends(the Quakers) setting the trends for decent employee treatment, many business magnates followed this example, and for that matter, Robert Owen's example, particularly from the year 1830 AD. Additionally, Parliamentary reforms, besides extending democratic rights for the British populace, established and refined the whole structure of local political bodies, charged with local responsibilities, with regard to education, roads and public amenities, and public social management where this was applicable. By the 1870s, large scaled businesses transgressed also into notable philanthropy, contributing vast amounts to the implementation – the finance and the support - of substantial municipal infrastructures, often on a par with the existing infrastructures of the Anglican and the Roman Catholic church organisations. In Bristol, Lilly, Wills & Company, which grew into W.D. & H.O. Wills by the year 1830 AD pioneered factory canteens, employee holidays and recreational facilities. By 1909 the Wills family chartered the formation of Bristol University with an initial donation of £100,000, and then subsequently through the years, completely financed the construction of the Wills Memorial building at the top of Park Street, and Bristol Museum, just further up the road at the Triangle. £110,000 and £25,000 were further donated by the Wills family for the construction of the university halls of residence for students. Considering the origins of the Wills business, local contentions have been expressed about its original ethics, using 'slave labour produced tobacco' with slave driven workers, to produce snuff and cigarettes for all of Britain's exploited workers, at least for fifty years or so, before factory scenes were improved during the latter end of the nineteenth century. Getting rich on it too. Although harsh, these comments are not without substance. One wonders whether really, the Wills's were stricken with guilt?

The problem was – even by the time Germany and Italy were born – that classic economic literary masters – such as 'John Stuart Mill', 'Adam Smith' and 'David Ricardo' - were exemplary icons of the establishment, much revered by the newspapers of the day. All amounted to a complete monopoly on economic thought in Britain, due really to the composition of the establishment, which – due to the prevailing 'undemocratic' nature of the British constitution – remained in the dark ages of the likes of 'Edmund Burke'. Distinctly biased to the 'right', in favour of the landed gentry and factory capitalists. Uncannily, the actions of a prominent convert to the concept of 'people power', and the literary outputs of a renowned political/economic/sociological philosopher, coincided by the year 1868 AD. William Gladstone – the great opponent of Benjamin Disraeli and queen Victoria – after rising to prominence as a Tory – with right wing leanings - by the year 1866 AD, jumped ship to lead the cause of the Liberal Parliamentary party, largely to accommodate all of the working minions that remained unrepresented. At that time, a lot of these existed in the British nation. With a mandate for significant changes to the constitution, he became the Prime Minister in the year 1868 AD in direct combat with Benjamin Disraeli, successfully superceding most of his doctrines by the year 1884 AD. During Gladstone's era, 'The Ballot Act'(1872) enabling secret political voting, 'The Reform Act'(1867) providing votes to workers residing in towns and cities, and 'The Reform Act(1884-5) providing votes to agricultural workers, and a framework of proportionate political constituencies, all came into being. At 'The Reform Act(1884-5) juncture, volume three of 'Das Capital' was also well on the way to completion. Actually completed in the year 1894 AD – making the whole of 'Das Capital' complete – the doctrines of Karl Marx arrived in the world, not only to oppose the old, crony concepts of John Stuart Mill, but also, to demolish the credentials of works like 'An Enquiry Into the Nature And Causes Of The Wealth of Nations', authored by Adam Smith in the preceding year 1776 AD.

Truly then, Britain came of age. Not only had it progressively improved the quality of life of all of its 'queen's subjects', it had improved the lot of many foreigners with the abolition of slavery, all while retaining and increasing economic prosperity. It had expanded its infrastructures, it had established a thriving merchant fleet and it had maintained a strong navy, to support and to safeguard a substantial empire in a volatile world. All really made possible by the sacrifices – and the enormous efforts – of robotised industrial workers – underling minions in their millions – blighted with disease, poverty and destitution at the dawn of the nineteenth century. Most of all, the sun shone on Britain and on all of its empire, because it provided opportunities for Karl Marx to record most of his clever notions in the midst of the text of 'Das Kapital'. Persecuted by the rising powers of Prussia and subsequently ejected from France, this German Jew of massive intellect found sanctuary in London's central library, enabling him to remain calm, peaceful and secure in mind. These ingredients were essential for the completion of his work. Regardless of all of the disrespectful propaganda that has been produced about him and Friedrich Engels – his socialist companion that financed him – in rag-tag newspapers – including 'The Daily Mail' particularly - most of the populations of the world – at one time or another – in China, particularly, in Russia particularly, in Vietnam particularly, in Nicaragua, in Spain(when the international army prevailed), in Chile, in Cuba particularly, in Venezuela, in Guatamalia, in Indonesia, and even in Granada, have adopted his philosophies, in preference to their national heritages. No other human being – other than successive Popes – has achieved world prominence to this extent. Least of all, all of the vehement advocators of the 'Holy Roman Empire'.

Section Thirty Eight:
Preludes Of The Great War

At the birth of 'Das Kapital', the poor and the destitutes of the world discovered a new idol to worship: Karl Marx, the 'people sharing' advocate.

Quite phenomenally, such worship extended the suffering of WW1. When Vladimir Lenin passed safely through Germany to his motherland in the year 1917 AD he – perhaps unwittingly – commenced the process of removing the military threat against Germany at its eastern borders, enabling the transfer of soldiers, to stiffen the western front, and thus to prolong the conflict. The Russian army on the eastern war front, flocked homewards in order to join the political revolution in its homeland, spurred very much by Lenin. Then, the volcano of Marxism erupted in all of the darkest echelons of the world, subsiding only with the fall of the 'Iron Curtain' – the German east/west wall, and the USSR – in the dwindling dusk of the twentieth century, after eighty years and more. Through it all, distinctively, the British establishment steered clear of Marxist philosophies, but in the end, it could not completely avoid the concepts of 'Socialism'.

Meanwhile, a strange connection appeared to exist between the classic philosophies of the German, Max Weber and the situation on the other side of the Atlantic ocean, in the north eastern regions of the USA. Numerous real-life examples appeared around the Pittsburg industrial belt just prior to – and just after – the birth of the twentieth century, that corroborated his contentions about business success correlating with religious fervour. Throughout the nineteenth century, similar examples had frequently appeared in Britain, also. Just as if the 16th century religious reformation from the 'Holy Roman Empire' had reverberated intensively through the subsequent centuries, with new religious factions breaking off the mainstream into all sorts of derivatives, increasingly pious, and therefore increasingly disciplined. Then by the time industrialism arrived in the world, the most holy christians in the thick of it – not of the catholic fraternity - were the ones that thrived. American industrialism, which was nurtured by many European immigrants with Protestant convictions, often sub-derived into Calvinism in particular, but also Quakerism, Methodism, Mennonitism, Hussitism, and very commonly with lots of Scots venturing then – as always – into north America, Presbyterianism. By the year 1857, Pittsburg featured over 1,000 factories, consuming twenty two million coal bushels yearly. Founded by many of the victims of the Merthyr Tydfil uprising that decided to try their luck in the 'New World', the Pittsburg industrial belt growth rate was phenomenal, not much hindered by the fire that destroyed over 1,000 buildings in the year 1845 AD. Spurred by a strong demand for weapons and military equipment during the civil war, and for railway rolling stock and tracks to span the great expanses of the land, British styled steel manufacturing evolved, big-time. Andrew Carnegie – a Scottish immigrant with a lot of industrial know-how, and with sharp business acumen – just rode along with it all, getting himself very wealthy in the process. Yet, Presbyterian Carnegie, from the start, never intended to retain such riches. Later after selling his vast interests in the Carnegie Steel Corporation in the year 1901, he gave all of his wealth away to all sorts of good causes.

Very coincidentally as it turned out, the peak of British industrial power – and the peak of its imperial power – was reached just as queen Victoria left the world, much to the relief of William Gladstone, but much to the regret of Empire exponents like Winston Churchill. Yet then, as one of the aristocracy, Churchill was hardly representative of the working underlings in Britain.

His father, Sir Randolph Churchill spent most of his later days at horse racing courses, and Winston was from birth, substantially endowed with wealth and with the glory, the extravagance – even the decadence – of the environs of Blenheim Palace in Oxfordshire. To this day, this is filled with enormous oil-painted art, typically of the battle of Blenheim(1704), hung as effigies of the glorious military legacy of the 'Duke of Marlborough' in the days when regents squabbled between themselves throughout the land of Europe 'to-be'. By the year 1906 AD however, these days were long gone. Winston Spencer Churchill's order of things was already extinct, although he didn't realise it at the time. At this juncture, a new Marxist inspired political force evolved – due to the efforts of Keir Hardie - in the form of the 'Labour Party', oriented much more to the left of the political spectrum than any other party, extremely so in comparison to the prevailing 'establishment', governed by Arthur Balfour between the years 1902 and 1905 AD. In comparison to the government of the 3rd Marquess of Salisbury – orchestrated mainly from the House of Lords between the years 1895 and 1902 – preceding Balfour's, Hardie's socialist advocates were like Martians in an alien world. In the midst of these times, Winston Churchill turned out to be a confusing character, indeed. Under Balfour's auspices – having managed to get himself elected to Parliament in the immediate wake of his pseudo heroism of the Boer war – he strangely opposed a principal political expedient, of profound significance that definitely contributed to the evolvement of WW1.

Section Thirty Nine:
Dreadnaughts Mania

By the year 1906 AD, the British navy – in the face of significant German colonial opposition, and in the midst of international territorial competition for African land – acquired a new military battleship named: 'Dreadnaught', which was really an improved derivative of the 'Satsuma', built in Britain and supplied to the Japanese navy by the end of the year 1905 AD. The lessons learned by the Russians during the Crimean war were duly expedited during subsequent Russian/Japanese confrontations, to which the Japanese navy soon worked to counteract, with ships like the 'Satsuma'. It appeared that the military demands of the day were for big battleships with big guns, to annihilate smaller opposition, and to bombard seashores from great distances. Within two years of the launch of 'Dreadnaught', the US navy also acquired the USS Michigan, built in the USA from Carnegie steel, of the same mould, but somewhat less advanced than the British versions; quite definitely slower with less armament. At that a juncture, US technology lagged behind that of Britain and Germany, but US industrial resources – particularly to produce war weapons – by the year 1906 AD was virtually on a par with both of these nations. Naturally, in the face of British naval supremacy, virtually throughout all of the oceans of the world, and in the midst of Germany's new-found confidence as a major industrial/colonial power in the world, manic battleship building by Britain and the USA inspired significant reciprocation.

Wikipeadia Extract – International Battleship Building Activities:

The first German response to Dreadnought came with the Nassau class, laid down in 1907. This was followed by the Helgoland class in 1909. Together with two battle cruisers - a type for which the Germans had less admiration than Fisher, but which could be built under authorisation for armoured cruisers, rather than capital ships - these classes gave Germany a total of ten modern capital ships built or building in 1909. While the British ships were somewhat faster and more powerful than their German equivalents, a 12:10 ratio fell far short of the 2:1 ratio that the Royal Navy wanted to maintain.

The battleship race soon accelerated once more, placing a great burden on the finances of the governments which engaged in it. The first dreadnoughts were not much more expensive than the last pre-dreadnoughts, but the cost per ship continued to grow thereafter. Modern battleships were the crucial element of naval power in spite of their price. Each battleship was a signal of national power and prestige, in a manner similar to the nuclear weapons of today. Germany, France, Russia, Italy, Japan and Austria all began dreadnought programs, and second-rank powers including the Ottoman Empire, Argentina, Brazil, and Chile commissioned dreadnoughts to be built in British and American yards.

In 1909, the British Parliament authorised an additional four capital ships, holding out hope Germany would be willing to negotiate a treaty about battleship numbers. If no such solution could be found, an additional four ships would be laid down in 1910. Even this compromise solution meant (when taken together with some social reforms) raising taxes enough to prompt a constitutional crisis in the United Kingdom in 1909–10. In 1910, the British eight-ship construction plan went ahead, including four Orion-class super-dreadnoughts, and augmented by battle cruisers purchased by Australia and New Zealand. In the same period of time, Germany laid down only three ships, giving the United Kingdom a superiority of 22 ships to 13. The British resolve demonstrated by their construction program led the Germans to seek a negotiated end to the arms race. While the Admiralty's new target of a 60% lead over Germany was near enough to Tirpitz's goal of cutting the British lead to 50%, talks foundered on the question on whether British Commonwealth battle cruisers should be included in the count, as well as non-naval matters like the German demands for recognition of ownership of Alsace-Lorraine.

The dreadnought race stepped up in 1910 and 1911, with Germany laying down four capital ships each year and the United Kingdom five. Tension came to a head following the German Naval Law of 1912. This proposed a fleet of 33 German battleships and battle cruisers, outnumbering the Royal Navy in home waters. To make matters worse for the United Kingdom, the Imperial Austro-Hungarian Navy was building four dreadnoughts, while the Italians had four and were building two more. Against such threats, the Royal Navy could no longer guarantee vital British interests. The United Kingdom was faced with a choice of building more battleships, withdrawing from the Mediterranean, or seeking an alliance with France. Further naval construction was unacceptably expensive at a time when social welfare provision was making calls on the budget. Withdrawing from the Mediterranean would mean a huge loss of influence, weakening British diplomacy in the Mediterranean and shaking the stability of the British Empire. The only acceptable option, and the one recommended by First Lord of the Admiralty Winston Churchill, was to break with the policies of the past and make an arrangement with France. The French would assume responsibility for checking Italy and Austria-Hungary in the Mediterranean, while the British would protect the north coast of France. In spite of some opposition from British politicians, the Royal Navy organised itself on this basis in 1912.

In spite of these important strategic consequences, the 1912 Naval Law had little bearing on the battleship force ratios. The United Kingdom responded by laying down ten new super-dreadnoughts in its 1912 and 1913 budgets - ships of the Queen Elizabeth and Revenge classes, which introduced a further step change in armament, speed and protection - while Germany laid down only five, concentrating resources on the Army.

United States:
The American South Carolina-class battleships were the first all-big-gun ships completed by one of the United Kingdom's rivals. The planning for the type had begun before Dreadnought was launched. While there is some speculation the U.S Navy design was influenced by informal contacts with sympathetic Royal Navy officials, the American ship was very different.

End Of Wikipeadia Extract - -- International Battleship Building Activities

Section Forty:
Hoodwinking Abound - The British Establishment Ignores Its Minions

Thus, four dominant 'war protagonising' nations – Britain, Germany, Japan and the USA - existed in the world, by 1913, of which Germany – in the middle of the European land mass – was most active, due largely to its new-found sovereignty and its accelerating industrial might, which produced all of the required resources for international expansionism. Within all four countries, war weapons production escalated out of control, even in the midst of widespread economic austerity. Where the 'establishments' of these nations pre-occupied themselves with international prestige – in the midst of nationalism ascendancy – all of their working underlings – their minions – sustained much increased taxation, to facilitate the expense of it all, without related prerogatives much to do with their disagreement of it. Looking at this situation retrospectively, with a new 'Labour' party formed in Britain by the year 1906 AD, it does not appear that the so-called new-found democracy in Britain and the USA – in particular, had much worth. This was so, because all of the 'establishments' of the advanced industrial nations of the world, had successfully filled the old ecclesiastic literature coffers, with 'establishment biased' newspapers whipping up national fervour all about, and with pro-establishment historic, political and economic authors vending all sorts of clever propaganda. During the process, all of the minions of these nations were truly 'hoodwinked'

By this juncture, most could read and write, but truth was denied them, keeping them all in ignorance of real world events. At local levels however, social eruptions were occurring. For example, during the year of 1910 AD, Winston Churchill involved himself with the placement of troops to establish order during the Tonypandy riots in Sales Wales, although at a later date, he contended that it was all a mix up. Earlier, he had been rejected for re-election to Parliament in the year 1905 AD, by his constituency party in Oldham, Lancashire. In reality, most of the working underlings in Britain were objecting to the 'establishment's' direction – which was mostly in contravention to their interests – but they remained impotent, in the midst of all of the prevailing 'Jingoism'. This direction headed affirmatively within a new sphere of international brinkmanship, towards astonishing extravagance, to devise, manufacture and to dangerously masquerade new weapons of war to unprecedented cost scales, of which – indirectly through taxation – all of the working minions sustained. Truly a manic endeavour, leading most of Europe – but actually, most of the minions of Europe – into Armageddon, as it turned out by the year 1914 AD.

Between the ages of six and eleven, I lived a solitary life at home, with a lovely Jack Russel bitch dog, some peanut butter and some bread in the larder, and with a television. Being motherless, most of the time my father was absent, in the day times and often in the evenings. Conspicuously, I hardly had any loyalties towards anyone. Much more profoundly maybe, I hardly had any idea about the differences between right and wrong. Much to my salvation however, I attended a very good primary school, still remembering the admirable head teacher – Mr Hall – to this day, through sixty years. Undoubtedly, without his sanction, I would have perished in one way or another. For me, the school holidays were another world however. In these times, my world comprised of peer wars, with occasional excursions to the Saturday morning cinema to watch 'The Three Stooges' and 'The Cyclopes'. All a bit vague now. Without parental guidance, I was not only a participant of gang battles – of which there were many within the open spaces of my council estate – but I was also prominent as an individual, in relation to tunnel digging, den building and boyhood bravado. In the midst of one of many of my fights with my 'council tenant' peers, the father of my opponent arrived on the scene, encouraging his son to 'be a man' and show me who was superior with his fists. Unperturbed, I understood even at that early age, that my opponent was dominated, lacking self-will to win. When all was over – inevitably to my gain – I experienced strong remorse for my opponent, not strangely anything to do with the injuries that I had inflicted upon him. All was much more to do with the humiliation that he experienced, accentuated enormously by his father's disappointment. At that time I realised that 'up' sides evolved from neglect.

Where my opponent lacked self-esteem and initiative, I was free-willed. Also fortunately, I was born with good capabilities. All of my peers wanted to accompany me in 'my' dens, and in 'my' tunnels, because they were better than theirs. In the days before I started to get out of control, my neglect and the related freedoms that it brought, suited me very much. Through it all, I only ever had 'one' faithful ally, accompanying me through all of my free time. Yet eventually, she paid for her loyalty to me with her life, after biting one of my fighting opponents on his nose, in response to my calls to her, to 'get him'. Then, I also realised just how unfair this world can be. Soon afterwards, I lost my dog, and I largely lost my freedoms, but by then, I had already vowed to myself, that I would never allow my father to dominate me, and from those times, he never did. Even with a strap around my buttocks, day in, day out, week in, week out. None of that sort of treatment ever worked. Amidst it all, there was something else that was strong and prominent within me. This was to do with the weakness of others. In opposition to me I found, that they sought the security of others like them. They established 'détentes' to exert their influence collectively, and thus, when multiple 'détentes' evolved in opposition, the phenomenon of 'gangs' became apparent. Not experiencing many limitations, rarely did I involve myself with these social structures. In a strange sort of way – due to my childhood neglect – I steered away from my father's communistic inclinations. Through storms and through tranquillity, I have been my own man, doing it all 'my way', for better of for worse. Lions ease their way through life without much individuality, but Cheetahs – as they pant with exhaustion – withhold their autonomomy.

Section Forty One:
The Great War – Between Establishments, But Not Between Minions

It was Africa, coupled with the insensitivity – of old – of the Hapsburg dynasty, the French and the Serbians that sewed the seeds of WW1. All substantially aided by the Russians and the British. Africa, being segmented into lots of irregular colonial satellites, bartered in the auctions of 'Entente Cordiale', settling Moroccan/Egyptian issues. France invading and annexing the Agadir vicinity of Morocco in the year 1911 AD in the face of German opposition, with Germany eventually somewhat compensated with a large chunk of the original French Congo. The Austrian-Hungarian Hapsburg empire annexing Bosnia-Herzegovina in the year 1908 AD. Serbia, with an officially sanctioned 'renegade' terrorist network, operating covertly with free licence, rather devastatingly assassinating 'Archduke Franz Ferdinand', the next presumed heir to the Austian-Hungarian-Hapsburg throne in the year 1914 AD. Serbia, infringing Hapsburg territory soon after the assassination incident, during the same year. Yet also, prominent descendents of the old 'Holy Alliance' of the year 1815 AD were implicated. Wilhelm 2nd of Prussia, the king of Germany, related to George 5th of the United Kingdom, in turn both related to Nicholas 2nd the Tsar of Russia. Truly the remnants of the old 'Holy Roman Empire', of which 'Archduke Franz Ferdinand' was a traditional affiliate. Put in this context, the remnants of the 'Holy Roman Empire' really sewed the seeds of WW1. With the Hapsburgs declaring war on Serbia soon after its territory was impinged upon, Tsar Nicholas – if he did but know then – signed his own death warrant by placing hundreds of thousands of Russian troops on the German and the Austrian borders, to ally with Serbia. By doing so, as a substantial war commenced, he drained his country of essential resources, in terms of materials and in terms of control. Duly exposing himself to the revolution that occurred in Russia by the year 1917 AD, which ultimately, invoked his assassination. All was pushed along by Keiser Wilhelm 2nd with Lenin's assisted transportation from Vienna to his homeland to join the rising Bolshevick movement.

With Russia substantially blockaded, Kaiser Wilhelm 2nd decided to gallivant through Belgium into France because he thought he could, as actually Hitler succeeded in doing during WW2. Then, it could be argued that imperialism knew no bounds. After all, Britain had recently marauded all about southern Africa in the process of the Boer war. The British during WW1, intervened – desperately and eagerly – principally to stem the growing strength of Germany, to retain the British Empire, inevitably to be threatened with German world dominance. All to acquiesce, with the independence of India by the year 1948 AD, and with the liberalisation of Africa and the far east by the early 1960s.

In the passing, the small matter of armaments expansion – really commencing before the turn of the century with the development of 'Dreadnaught' styled naval capabilities – evolved into ordinance megalomania, in the thick of which the likes of H.H. Kitchener played with British minions – brainwashed, ignorant underlings and brainwashed aristocrats even – as if they were all Turkeys in a Christmas line of execution. By the year 1916 – with all of the new Armageddon fully raging – William Maxwell Aitken(Lord Beaverbrook) had arrived in Britain – armed with '*Ottmar Mergenthaler's' hot metal 'linotype' technology in hand – to exuberate all of the killing capers in the 'Daily Express', 'The 'Sunday Express' and the 'Evening Standard' newspapers. 'Jingoism' just bounced around everywhere in Britain, to support H.H. Kitchener's "Your country needs you" campaign.

Paradoxically though, Beaverbrook's newspapers – and a lot of the unofficial grapevine – rang alarm bells in the minds of the 'unconvinced', who had chosen not to volunteer for military service during the initial phase. With French front-line troops mutinying, with Krupp artillery demolishing virtually all of Belgium and northern France, and with new

German 'U Boats' virtually nullifying the power of all of the glorious 'Dreadnaught' styled battleships, volunteers to fight on the war front vapourised like water in a steaming kettle. Inevitably, all of the minions that were fit enough to fight fell into the fold of 'military conscription', big time. Just as before within Britain's horrid industrial scene of old, so did all of the poor old horses. All to their demise in the biggest slaughtering domain, that had ever existed in the world, throughout all of the millennia preceding that time. Even colonial Canadians, Australians, New Zealanders(collectively ANZACS), Senegalese, Sheiks, Indians and Celonese, and especially, Welsh miners that dug tunnels under 'no-mans-land' to place deadly explosives under German trenches. Imperialism knew no bounds then, least of all the limits of human decency, in the midst of strong establishment exponents, many of whom were found in the Prussian camp. With 250,000 fatalities during the early campaign of the Dardinelles, the overall fatality statistics are stupendous. To the disappointment of football enthusiasts, whether or not a football match – of any substance – took place on the first Christmas day of the war, remains unsubstantiated, although numerous ambiguous records of its mention exist. Definitely though, opposing troops – along several sections of the front – generated Christmas 'goodwill' relations between themselves by exchanging gifts. More particularly, it is substantiated that they shared their common 'Holy Roman Empire' heritage, by singing hymns communally from the trenches and in the middle of no-mans-land. Strong gestures of peace, accompanied by – according to numerous testaments – expressions of 'a reluctance to fight'. These activities were definitely widespread on that day, although the popularity of specific hymns – of which there existed commonality – varied between sides. All suggesting affirmatively, that WW1 was not a conflict much desired by the underlings – the minions – of Europe. It was really a war between establishments, with a few old-styled regencies thrown in, to-boot.

However, WW1 has been documented – and pontificated about – more than enough to absolve the need for much consideration on this matter, here, with the exception of the notable facts that follow. French and German national prestige slumped to devastating depths by the end of it all, principally because of the French military mutinies and because of Germany's defeat. For the first time ever, national entities – Britain, France, Russia and Germany – found themselves in states of desperate destitution. That is to say: all of the lowly minions within these nations, although the Russian peasantry found a new social identity in the midst of Bolshevikism. Also notably, the pinnacle of German aristocracy – Kaiser Wilhelm 2nd, with all of his entourage – ceased to be, enabling Germany to function as a republic, albeit weak and useless in subsequent years. In the meantime, relating to Britain and northern France, thousands upon thousands of war survivors perished before the 1920s decade arrived, as a consequence of a massive influenza pandemic, which really, need not have occurred to the scale that it did. Discounting this event, very large portions of originally 'fit' men ceased to be by the end of the conflict, throughout Europe, inclusive of Russia. The young European generation of this time was truly decimated. In fact, in human kind terms, the whole of Europe had transposed into a pitiful sacrificial pig; all for nothing, except for significant technological advancement. In all, WW1 – the mother of all wars – discounting influenza pandemic fatalities, took sixteen million lives, many of which from Britain, did not even hold an entitlement to vote because they were under twenty one years of age. Old enough to fight, suffer and to die at eighteen years, but not old enough for political involvement in their nation.

Section Forty Two:
British Women Acclaimed

The real irony was, that many sixteen and seventeen year olds – who lied about their ages – contributed to the mortality figures. Astonishingly – not by accident or even by neglect, but by design – 'all' of the womenfolk of Britain – whether lowly or aristocratic – along with all of the men that were deprived of property ownership – could not be counted in any sort of political power tallies, to the year 1918 AD. All of the poor men dodging artillery shells and machine gun bullets, and all of the women, most of whom had abandoned their kitchens – and even their children often – to slave and to strive in war weapons production environs, for 'the national effort', not for lucrative payment. All caused social fragmentation in the wake of the war, due to the 'men' survivors, who wished to return to their pre-war employment, thus to banish the women back to their kitchens. Not as much fragmentation, as probably would have occurred without parliamentary legislation to remedy the prevailing feminine deprivations, commenced and concluded in the House of Commons by November of the year 1918 AD, and subsequently into law before the general election in the December of that year. This new law – operating under the auspices of the Representation of the People act(1918), provided political involvement with the right of a 'vote' in national elections for all women of the age of thirty and over, who 'owned property'. Yet really from the year 1912 AD, significant social unrest and social fragmentation inspired by the likes of Emmeline Pankhurst – the widow of the feminist pioneer Richard Pankhurst – had occurred successively, in the midst of an ongoing 'female emancipation' campaign. Soon after her declaration of extreme militancy in the year 1912 AD, Emmeline was arrested twelve times, most prolifically as an arsonist.

With the advent of the Russian revolution – with riots on the streets of Mosow, and with all of the worries of WW1 – the suppression of this disruption was imperative in the minds of Parliamentarians, recently witnessing the abandonment of the war by thousands of Russian soldiers. In this context, the granting of 'the vote' to propertied women in Britain in the year 1918 AD – before the official end of WW1 – was not a reward for all of the effort that they had expended, though the removal of the property qualification for men – also included in the act – was. Particularly, fighting men of the age of nineteen years, also gained a vote, where the general qualification remained at twenty one years. Realistically, the vote was given to the women of Britain at that juncture – where French women remained disfranchised for numerous years later – as a strategy of appeasement, with the government of the day running scared, due to previous disruption. In the strongest of terms, this event set a precedent, of dastardly character and of devious nature, inherent and prominent now within the framework of government within Britain. Particularly conspicuous from the 1960s era, onwards. Really, 'electorate appeasement' is a 'Roman Emperor' tactic of old, gaining prominence most often during troubled times. Keep the people happy. Build the coliseums and bring out the gladiators. See it now in the year 2015 AD, in the wake of the 'Scottish Independence' vote. Such was an enormous concession however, much to the dislike of Tory Lord Curzons, then. The constitutional structure of the country altered radically, with the electorate composition tripling from 7.7 million to 21.4 million, with women comprising 43% of the total vote in the election of the year 1918 AD. If the women's vote had not been restricted to thirty years and over(owning property), then more women – many more – than men, would have been qualified to vote, due to the British male fatalities of WW1.

Of all of the participating belligerent nations of WW1, one winner evolved: the USA. US eastern economies derived enormous economic benefits much before the entry of US military forces into the WW1 arena, which was during the summer of the year 1918 AD. The range – and the ferocity – of fighting, placed logistic demands on the allied forces, much beyond their supply capabilities. In this context, WW1 was not a war of spasmodic heroes. Nor was it an arena of stupendous heroism. Decisively, Hiram Maxim's 'machine gun' – invented and deployed in time for the Paschendale slaughter, and the like – totally nullified broad in-line advances by foot soldiers, and so did barbed wire. Fighting was often more about holding a Le-Enfield .303 rifle steady, to sharpshoot, or to pincer attack within new – precarious - moving armoured 'tanks', to spread 'machine-gun' fodder in the midst of the enemy. WW1 was most definitely, a war of attrition, decided eventually – inexorably – by logistics, and opposing troop strengths, in terms of numbers. With France's – and even Britain's – industrial capabilities depleted substantially by the year 1918 AD, American east coast economies – much geared upwards to supply the fighting allies in Europe – advanced and expanded to new economic dimensions. Slowing somewhat in the wake of initial advancements after the civil war, the American economy experienced a renaissance by the year 1916 AD, retained and consolidated after all of the European fighting was over, through to the late 1920s.

Section Forty Three:
The Eventual Demise Of The USA – European Destitution

In war front terms, with US involvement in WW1, the price that it paid for this economic rejuvenation was: 110,000 men lost in combat, and a further 43,000 men, that succumbed to the Influenza pandemic. Which – within the grand scale of things, comparatively – was not a lot. However, if General Pershing had not been such a buffoon, less deaths would have occurred. Initially, his men were fodder for machine-guns, advancing in-line. Significantly, with German/Allied forces equally spent by the summer of the year 1918 AD, US incursions into the fighting sphere, definitely tipped the balance in the Allies's favour. As of old – in compliance with the follies of Napoleon Bonaparte during the year 1812 AD – grand scaled wars were decided by resources, not by heroism. With the circumstantial arrival of the internal combustion engine in the world, just twenty or so years prior to WW1, and with the fragile birth of aviation – with aspects of it developing even during the conflict – the pace of technological change in the world 'spring boarded' to new 'mega' dimensions, within just one decade of the precarious peace that followed. Even before this period – but also, especially because of WW1 – Henry Ford(in America), William Morris(in Britain) and Karl Benz of Mercedes Benz(in Germany) transposed the suffering of many of the poor horses in this world, into embryos of motorised mechanisation. Immediately in the USA, but not for a while in Europe or in Russia. Within these domains, the small matter of destitution relief took precedence.

Yet, it did not realistically occur. The emaciated domain of Europe festered, especially in Germany, but also in Italy, in Spain, in France and in Britain, with all of the underling minions of these nations persistently grovelling for subsistence. Contrastingly in the USA, with industrialism duly rejuvenated due to the initial demands of WW1, and with a vast land mass filled with a diversely inspired populace - yet to be filled with suitable infrastructures, especially appertaining to shipping and motor transport - the economy expanded and thrived. Some aspects of which reverberated within wealthy European circles, not always in a detrimental way. In the immediate wake of WW1, the millionaire Albert Kahn despatched a team of photographers throughout the world to capture dying cultures for his magnificent 'Autochrome' collection. Charles Lindberg flew the Atlantic Ocean alone, and the wealthy in England jumped onto the 'Charleston' bandwagon, often literally. By the year 1921 AD however, disaster loomed in Germany, where truly, economic war recovery had not been realised to any measure. Most of the employers of the minions there were existing on the back of short-term – high interest – American loans, which were re-called – without renewal privileges – when France occupied the German industrial Rhineland district of Westfalia in the year 1923 AD, as a reprisal for Germany's refusal to pay WW1 reparations.

Preceding this event, the German Weimar government raised the funds to pay reparations by increasing its Fiduciary Issue. 'Quantitive Easing' in today's jargon, which really means: printing paper money, without corresponding resources – typically gold – to back it. Then it exchanged this new money into foreign currency to pay the reparations. Subsequently, the German deutschmark progressively diminished in value until the situation was reached where Germany could not keep paying, by the year 1923 AD. When France occupied the Rhineland, the German deutschmark devalued even more extensively on the foreign exchange markets. To exasperate the problem, the German government printed even more worthless paper money, to pay the wages of striking miners in the Rhineland, acting in opposition to the French occupation. Between June 1922 and December of the same year, the cost of living index in Germany rose from 41 to 685, which was a fifteen fold increase. At the beginning of the year 1922 AD, one American dollar was worth DM320. By June, the same year, the American dollar was worth DM800. At the juncture of the recall of the American short-term loans – which was a consequence of the downfall of the German mark – the working employment scene in Germany dissolved into chronic slump. Most of the minions starved.

In the meantime, Winston Churchill – rejoining the Conservative party as the Chancellor of the Exchequer in Britain by the year 1924 AD – somewhat baffled by all of the economic intricacies in Germany, followed his 'Dumbkoff' nose – running scared – and returned Britain to the old 'Gold Standard', with gold in the Bank of England to match every new £ - pound – issued. He adopted this stance, even after receiving opposing advice from John Maynard Keynes(the world's greatest economist of the time). Yet really, this 'Gold Standard' thing was just one component of an enormous strategy of austerity, implemented by Churchill, which inevitably brought about the general slump and the consequent 'General Strike' in the year 1926 AD. All of which fostered national trade rivalry – with the placement of a lot of import tariffs – throughout all of Europe. Having acted to accelerate the demise of all of the working minions in Britain with strict economic austerity – which did not affect his own wealthy circumstances - Churchill was reported to have suggested that: "machine guns be used on the striking miners". At the time, he edited the Government's newspaper, the British Gazette, and during the dispute he argued that "either the country will break the General Strike, or the General Strike will break the country", further claiming that the fascism of Benito Mussolini "rendered a service to the whole world, showing a way to combat subversive forces". He considered the regime to be a bulwark against the perceived threat of communist revolution. At one point, Churchill went as far as to call Mussolini the "Roman genius ... the greatest lawgiver among men".

Wikipeadia Extracts: About Winston Churchill

In March of the year 1916 AD, Churchill returned to England after he had become restless in France and wished to speak again in the House of Commons. Future prime minister David Lloyd George acidly commented: "You will one day discover that the state of mind revealed in (your) letter is the reason why you do not win trust even where you command admiration. In every line of it, national interests are completely overshadowed by your personal concern." In the July of the year

1917 AD, Churchill was appointed Minister of Munitions, and in the January of the year 1919 AD, Secretary of State for War and Secretary of State for Air. He was the main architect of the Ten Year Rule, a principle that allowed the Treasury to dominate and control strategic, foreign and financial policies under the assumption that "there would be no great European war for the next five or ten years". A major preoccupation of his tenure in the War Office was the Allied intervention in the Russian Civil War. Churchill was a staunch advocate of foreign intervention, declaring that Bolshevism must be "strangled in its cradle". He secured, from a divided and loosely organised Cabinet, intensification and prolongation of the British involvement beyond the wishes of any major group in Parliament or the nation - and in the face of the bitter hostility of Labour. In the year 1920 AD, after the last British forces had been withdrawn, Churchill was instrumental in having arms sent to the Poles when they invaded Ukraine. He was also instrumental in having para-military forces (Black and Tans and Auxiliaries) intervene in the Irish War of Independence. He became Secretary of State for the Colonies in the year 1921 AD and was a signatory of the Anglo-Irish Treaty of the year 1921 AD, which established the Irish Free State. Churchill was involved in the lengthy negotiations of the treaty and, to protect British maritime interests, he engineered part of the Irish Free State agreement to include three Treaty Ports - Queenstown, Berehaven and Lough Swilly - which could be used as Atlantic bases by the Royal Navy. In the year 1938 AD, however, under the terms of the Chamberlain-De Valera Anglo-Irish Trade Agreement, the bases were returned to Ireland.

End of Wikepeadia Extracts – Winston Churchill

Interestingly, after Churchill unwittingly frenzied the underling minions of Britain, year on year, with his: 'the aristocracy is supreme' rhetoric, he and his principal accomplice Stanley Baldwin, were forced to declare a state of emergency in the midst of the 'General Strike' of the year 1926 AD. Yet very soon afterwards, both headed in the direction of appeasement – rather faced with situations they could not handle – by augmenting the existing 'Representation of the People act in the year 1928 AD. Struggling to get back into favour, they removed the existing restrictions on women's votes, to enable them to behave like proper adults at the age of twenty one years(without property qualifications), instead of thirty years(with property qualifications). Truly an extension of the pioneering appeasements of the year 1918 AD, many of a similar nature would follow. Even now, rumour pervades about sixteen year olds acquiring the vote. Where the situation in Britain was dire under Churchill's auspices, all should now be grateful that he did not turn out to be a dictator, of the nature of Benedito Mossolini, who by the year 1922 AD in Italy arrived on the political scene, ultimately to quell – by force and bludgeon in the end – all of the disgruntlements of his compatriots. We all know now, of his dealings to make them all subordinate underlings, with all of the ramifications that this implies. Strangely, while active, he left the principal old Italian dynasties in place. Namely, the king Victor Emmanuel 3rd and 'The Papacy'. Victor Emmanuel was realistically nullified however, acting as his puppet until the year 1943 AD. Then he disassociated himself, with hopes of regency revival. Quite to the contrary, when all of the chaos and the turmoil of WW2 was over, the relatively new nation of Italy established itself as a true democratic republic in the year 1946 AD. During Mossolini's heyday, the new nation of 'The Vatican' was born, principally to confine the Papacy within the defined bounds of 'The Vatican See', as an alternative to permitting the Papacy to range all about Rome, as it had since it moved from Avignon in the fourteenth century. The ramifications of WW1 depleted themselves much slower however in France.

Section Forty Four:
Spain And Poland Compared

Remarkably, its minions held on to its third republic without extreme upheavals. Least of all, the French needed another. Yet the infrastructure repair and replacement task was daunting, in the midst of austerity. Everybody knows where the German situation went to in the wake of the collapse of the Veimar Republic. The details of which are not dealt with within this text. Characteristically, the slowest to respond to the prevailing hardships of the age, Spain, evolved into a tumultuous catastrophe for democratic exponents, which to this day has not been resolved completely. That is to say, a proper democratic republican structure is not yet evident, and that frictions and agitations – in addition to devolvement inclinations – to this end, prevail. What a travesty the Spanish story is? The only consolation to its traditionalists is the current success of its football teams, both regional and national. As the second republic commenced its second term, 'the Butcher of Asturias' – General Franco – invoked a coup d'etat in the year 1936 AD, just as if he was some sort of heralding exponent of the 'Holy Roman Empire'. All about Spain during the first electoral term of the republic, the unofficial – illegal – will of many of the people was expressed, with many arson attacks on

Roman Catholic churches, even after the government of the first term had legislated to prohibit ecclastic influence within educational spheres. Simultaneously in the year 1933 AD, it imposed stringent controls on all of the Papacy's Spanish properties. Duly, Franco's coup d'etat failed, but he controlled all of Spain's armies.

Cleverly, most of the troops from Spain's Moroccan colony were extricated to support Franco's cause, and so commenced a vicious civil war – originally emanating from modest 'Falange' incursions in the north and the south west regions of Spain - raged for more than three years, with approximately 500,000 deaths as the result, many of which occurred in dastardly fashions. In the midst of this scenario, the World experienced the wrath of Adolf Hitler for the first time. The Spanish conflict was his testing ground for his embryonic army, and many of his new weapons of war. Then it turned out, that 'The National Socialist' party in Germany – headed by the Nazis – was not socialist at all; it was distinctly fascist, aligning with and supporting General Franco. All of which turned out to be decisive, even with a dedicated – if somewhat disorganised – internationally composed military contingent – in the name of the renowned 'International Brigade' - supporting the forces of the legitimate government. Really, where Neville Chamberlain – the British Prime Minister in this era – was forced to face up to Hitler by the year 1939 AD – with the commencement of the Nazi invasion of Poland – the British government wrongly dissolved inclinations to – militarily - support the legitimate Spanish government. Indifference to the Spanish, and then compassion for the Polish; why? Because in the face of the ascendancy of communism in Russia, Poland – newly created by the allies at the conclusion of

WW1 – was much more representative of the values and virtues of its allies, to its west, inclusive of Britain, than Spain. All really, was about perpetuating the archaic 'Holy Roman Empire'/Monarchical structure, which was prominent in Poland then. From its inception in the year 1919 AD, to its invasion by the Russian army in the year 1945 AD, aristocracy prominence and class distinction in Poland was rife. All of which was supported with a substantially strong Jewish community. Then ominously, Auchwitz evolved.

By which time, the bastions of the age-old order of things in Britain – coincidentally enjoying political power – were speaking in public vigorously in their interests, not to get involved with Spain's turmoil. To this aim, they were also 'old-boy-networking' to generate perpetual 'hoodwink' styled newspaper headlines, virtually to damnate Spanish republican efforts. Characteristically, the related early Nazi belligerence was placed in a vacuum void, hardly ever reported. Worse, by the time the real crunch occurred – with the invasion of Poland – the relatively new technology of radio was enjoying prolific usage. The Prime Minister – in a cloak of extraordinary importance then, Neville Chamberlain – was able to broadcast all of the justifications of his actions – without due opposition – to all of his 'ignorant' underlings. Then, with the progression of the Hitler phenomenon, his successor, Winston Churchill, pioneeringly utilised this media to deliver all of his 'death or glory' speeches, which realistically grasped all of the hearts and minds of the minions of Britain, to wage war on Germany. "We shall fight in the air, and on the beaches, etc", and so they all did, like it or not. Consequent conscription was universal. Through all of this however – and through all of the austerity newspaper propaganda of the Churchill kind that preceded the WW2 declaration – the underling's 'grapevine' retained functionality, effectively counter-acting many of the formal dictates. At the peak of the Spanish civil war in 1936-7, big trouble was afoot within the domain of all of Britain's working underlings, situated mostly in the north of the country. Where Neville Chamberlain had done much to raise living standards within the middle-class conurbations of the south, his government virtually neglected – in the midst of dire poverty and destitution – the real 'grafters' of Britain in the north. Then, the children of coal miners scurried around on slag-heaps for fuel to keep themselves warm, and 'out-of' work' ship builders marched a thousand miles to protest at Westminster, from Jarrow. When these kinds eventually went to fight in WW2, they went reluctantly, with a substantial amount of knowledge – acquired through the 'grapevine' – that inclined them to think that they were being usurped to fight for the wrong reasons. Meanwhile, Churchill's lot augmented their propaganda machine with 'Pathe Newsreels' at cinemas, much designed to brainwash all of the underling suckers.

Ominously, the American post WW1 heyday culminated into a disaster to world dimensions by the year 1929 AD, with a Wall Street stock market crash, which turned out to be the 'mother of all', until another one arrived in the 1990s decade, serious enough to exterminate 'Leaman Brother Incorporated'. Economic growth which had been spurred with the advancement of technologies, to supply the allies in WW1, and to expand the whole of America's transport infrastructure, subsisted with substantial reductions in demand. The American home market was saturated, and the rest of the world was still destitute. Thus, exporting potentials were not evident. Importantly, while the likes of Henry Ford were preparing to down-scale their phenomenal production outputs, serious droughts occurred successively in the American mid-west, stemming agricultural production to drastic proportions. In short, while criminality exploded in the land free of the 'Holy Roman Empire' legacy, the whole world was bankrupt. The 'Mafia', by now well contained in Italy, experienced a renaissance in the USA, due ironically to the agitations and the puritanical protestations of the Protestant motivated 'Women's Christian League', in the midst of universal alcohol prohibition. By the year 1934 AD, Al Capone had been and gone, and many federal US states were experiencing the criminal holocaust of Bonnie and Clyde and John Dillinger, all of whom were notorious murderers, driven initially by poverty. Truly, the flourishing times of types like J. Edgar Hoover of the American FBI(Federal Bureau of Investigation), with all that this implied.

It is these factors now that bring me to thoughts about my own life, especially during the very early stages of it. I remember listening to my father's brother, Jack – who turned out to be a better father to me, than my own – about his early childhood, beginning in the year 1928 AD. By the year 1935 AD he was old enough to remember the extended absence of his mother – my Daintee toffy worker grandmother – in a world then that supplied hardly any food. When he told me initially, these comments meant nothing, but now – knowing the history of the age – I realise the extent of the hardships that existed then. By the time that he and his brothers reached adulthood, they were all packed off into the military, to be ready for war, but by this time, it was nearly concluded. What came out of it all, counting their upbringings and their brief military experiences was a distinct appreciation of the hardships and the fears of those times. You see – coupled with all of this – I learned of Clyde Barrow's penal experiences before he evolved into a notorious gangster: he had been seriously brutalised in prison, at the start of his criminal career. Contentions prevail nowadays about how such brutalisation sews the seeds of violent criminality; often applied to the Barrow phenomenon. Then I considered: 'Why do brutes brutalise?' Within formal settings, in my opinion – completely unqualified though – brutality is often a malignancy of misguided self righteousness. A kind of adulterated piousness with incredible justifications for all sorts of detrimentally extreme actions. On playing in a sand pit near to my home at an age of five years or so, a man walked by me clicking a child's play cap gun. I looked at him, and he looked at me, then he gave it to me kindly before continuing on his way. Why did my elder half-sister – who knew that my father was a brute with a belt – after seeing me with the toy, run off home to tell him of my new possession, just as soon as she could?

Then, why – after making me stand immediately in front of him with my trousers down – did my father whip me with his heavy belt, every time that I answered his: "Where did you get it?" question with: "A man gave it to me". That session lasted a very long time, painfully. In the end I lied to stop the torture, and from that day, never did I speak to him with the truth. Come to think of it, I hardly spoke the truth to anyone else, either, for years, and years. Additionally, I was so materially deprived during my upbringing, as to steal anything of worth that was not bolted down. Massive modelling kits from Woolworths, without a qualm or care. Finally, after searching for my uncle Jack in Birmingham after hitch-hiking from Cardiff, I drove away – never having driven anything before – a commercial van, which had been left unattended with its ignition keys in place. Then more by accident than by design, I played ricochet down the urban streets of Birmingham, with all of the parked vehicles. Yet as a consequence, the police and the magistrates in the juvenile court, placed faith in me. They believed me about my pending entry into the Royal Air Force as a boy and they set me free with faith, and with the belief that I could make good. Duly, given decent sanctuary within the Royal Air Force, still as a boy of sixteen years, I did. Comparatively so, anyway. Of my father? He is dead and gone, not missed much. Of my elder half-sister? She has proved herself a villain on numerous occasions: dumped into oblivion now.

Section Forty Five:
The Ominous Iron Curtain – Of Churchill's Making

I have subsequently discovered that the 1930s decade was probably the most notable of all, since the year 1066 AD. For the first time ever, serious attempts to exterminate religion and royal regencies – all of which really constituted the 'Holy Roman Empire' – occurred in Spain – spurred by the Russian 'revolution' phenomenon – and in Germany with the prevalence of the Nazis. Widely diverse in relation to their overall objectives and their ideals - in the midst of the prelude years of WW2 - Russia, Spain and Germany pursued this expedient commonly. At the start of the decade, the impending trends riveted all of the existing royal regencies of Europe. In the year 1931 AD, king Alfonso 13th of Spain was removed from power as democracy evolved. With the ascendancy of Benidito Mossolini in Italy, the Papacy sat fretting – eventually blessing him for his salvation – and king Victor Emmanuel 3rd made himself very inconspicuous, only to fall in the end. Additionally – due to severe economic circumstances – in the northern regions of Britain, rebellion fermented in the face of Winston Churchill styled rule, with all of its bluster about the preservation of the British Empire, and the British royals. All reached a crescending climax with the abdication of king Edward 8th at the climax of the Spanish civil war in the year 1936. By then, Kim Philby, Guy Burgess, Donald McClean and Anthony Blunt were active as clandestine agents for the Russian establishment, with their American associate Henry Angleton, tearing his hair out in the midst of all of the treachery. With Hitler's annexations of 'The Rhineland', 'Sudetenland' and then the whole of 'Czechoslovakia', with Mossolini well entrenched, and with General Franco firmly placed, Europe transposed nearer to dictatorial Hell, and truly, by the time Neville Chamberlain mobilised troops for the defence of Norway against Hitler, it had entered the depths of Armageddon, just to escape eventually, due principally to Napoleon Bonaparte's foe of folly, of old: the mass of the lands, the ferocity of weather and the population enormity of Russia. Not forgetting of course, the magnificence of all of the other European minions of that age, regardless of their alliances and their loyalties. After all, they were just lowly underlings, trying to make the best of their circumstances, without their own control over them, and most of the time, without the Pope to pray for them. Not that most of them cared much about that.

Rather profoundly though – spurred by the successive wars of WW1 and WW2, technology in the world accelerated in leaps and bounds, to unprecedented dimensions. Frighteningly, within the bounds of the new nuclear destruction phenomenon, the successful belligerents of WW2 – the USA, Britain and Russia, with France trumpeting to join them – clouded the vanquished, all pervasively. Militarily and culturally, the prevailing nuclear bomb threat determined the overall way of things, and thus Churchill's 'iron curtain' evolved as a new myth – much created by his own political actions – to foster the prevalence of 'The Cold War'. Of all of the damnation of the 'Cambridge Spies' of Britain, the real Armageddon that did arrive in the world – in Japan, at Hiroshama and Nagasaki – was stemmed by them. Kim Philby's and Donald McClean's success – in collusion with the German Klaus Fuchs – in feeding atomic bomb 'know-how' information to the Russians, suppressed the possible evolvement of 'world domination' megalomania. By the year 1948 AD, the Russian atomic bomb arrived, to establish temporarily, political equilibrium in the world. Since, Europe has lived in peace. The British queen and the Pope are still around, but, but, but........? All is another story to be told. Meanwhile - more dreadfully perhaps? – certainly since the Boer war, in the west of Europe and in the USA, all of the minions became much more literally capable, to become more informed about events. In the subsequent WW2 era, all was augmented profoundly, with the arrival of 'Television', thus facilitating – greatly – 'widespread' propaganda, initially controlled strictly in Britain through the auspices of the 'British Broadcasting Corporation'. Paradoxically then, all of the less ignorant minions – who could read and who could analyse more capably - were further indoctrinated with more biased information, just because nationally directed control mechanisms – radio, television, newspapers and school teaching – worked perversely to conceal all of the real facts that substantiated opposing ideologies. Ironically, the improvements in education achieved during the 20th century to that time, enabled 'the establishment' to propagate its pro-establishment dictums, more profusely and more convincingly, than ever before. Yet, at the time of the first Russian atomic bomb explosion, Winston Churchill and his entourage – with all of their 'Iron Curtain' exasperations – fell dumb with impotence. Most of the young men of Britain – in the mayhem of WW2 – had newly experienced prominent social class divisions, and lots of deaths, and severe austerity; the perils of military engagement set aside. Many professed: "Let India have its independence. 'To-Hell' with the Empire and Churchill". Very deservingly instead, they were all provided with a new 'free at the point of need' national health service.

Without much care by British underling minions at that time, a long wall appeared through the centre of Berlin, augmented with a fence crossing the whole of Germany by the year 1961 AD. In reality, Churchill's speech of his 'Iron Curtain' myth – given in the land of his mother's birth, at Fulton, USA – in the year 1946 AD, sewed the seeds of western belligerence, which in turn, exacerbated the precariousness of shared political power in Berlin, resulting in the 'Berlin Airlift' political confrontation between Russia, the USA, and Britain. Conspicuously, France – an included power sharer in Berlin at the time - did not much involve itself with this affair. By the time that John F. Kennedy appeared on the political scene in America, General De Gaulle – who had already drawn swords with Churchill, Roosevelt and

General Eisenhower – retracted France from the American led military coalition of NATO(North Atlantic Treaty Organisation), subsequently adopting a policy of 'détente' with so-called Iron Curtain countries in the east of Europe. With his neutrality stance during the Vietnam war, his opposition to all of the American led anti-Soviet belligerence leading to the erection of the walls and the fences in Germany, was clearly demonstrated. To all of which, Winston Churchill was the archetype conspirator.

Made in the USA
Charleston, SC
19 February 2015